Chic
on a
Shoestring

Chic
on a
Shoestring

Simple to sew vintage-style accessories

Mary Jane Baxter

Photography by Claire Richardson

Illustrations by Sam Wilson

Kyle Books

To Maureen and Peter Baxter with grateful love from their daughter Mary Jane

First published in Great Britain in 2011 by
Kyle Books
an imprint of Kyle Cathie Ltd
23 Howland Street
London, W1T 4AY
www.kylebooks.com

ISBN: 978 1 85626 981 0

A CIP catalogue record for this title is available from the British Library

10 9 8 7 6 5 4 3 2

Design: Louise Leffler
Photography: Claire Richardson
Illustrations: Sam Wilson
Project editor: Sophie Allen
Copy editor: Anna Hitchin
Production: Sheila Smith and Nic Jones

Colour reproduction by
Sang Choy
Printed and bound by
Toppan Leefung Printing
Ltd in China

Contents

introduction

If you're anything like me, you'll know how it feels to gaze longingly at enticing images in glossy magazines and realise that the object of your desire is way beyond your reach. There's the handcrafted necklace that'll mean an overdraft, the stunning shoes that will deprive you of your rent or the elegant hat that'll blow your credit rating out of the water. But it doesn't have to be like that.

Chic on a Shoestring is the doorway to a different world, one in which your creativity will flourish and your purse strings won't snap. Leaf through the pages and you'll find a plethora of ingenious ideas for transforming stuff you might otherwise throw out or ignore into a closet full of covetable clothes and accessories.

Inspired by Claire Richardson's stunning photographs and aided by Sam Wilson's delightful illustrations, I'll give you step-by-step instructions to show you how you too can become your own makeover magician using basic sewing techniques. If you're a beginner, you'll relish being able to achieve stunning results without accumulating a vast array of skills and equipment; if you're already an accomplished seamstress you'll find a host of fresh and exciting projects as well as possibilities for stamping them with your own personality.

Chic on a Shoestring will change your look from top to toe. There's the charming pillbox hat conjured from a cereal box, the shoelaces that become a show-stopping choker, the silk scarf that emerges as a seductive summer top and the brogues that bring to life your basic lace-ups. There are tips for embellishing and customising everyday clothes to help you express your signature style whether it's vintage or modern, and a guide to finding those treasured bits and pieces to incorporate into your designs.

I mostly stitch by hand, which means that lots of the 'makes' are portable and perfect for long train journeys or boredom-inducing commutes. Besides, I've always found that people love it when you stitch in public, and I've discovered it often helps break down barriers and forge new friendships. Occasionally I suggest using a sewing machine. Often it's because I want a more robust finish, or feel it's a bit faster. But to be honest, you could complete nearly everything in this book entirely by hand if you wanted to.

As I'm rather impatient myself, you'll find that many of the items in the book can be completed in under an hour and none should take more than an afternoon or evening. There are no complicated patterns, just some easy-to-trace templates to help you get things right.

For those of you for whom sewing is still a bit of a mystery, or for 'chiconomistas' who want to leave their needle and thread behind for a change, I've also included some no-sew suggestions that I hope will banish for good the impression that craft and fashion cannot be friends.

Most of all though, this book is about indulging your creative side, having fun and making beautiful, timeless pieces that you'll want to wear again and again. I hope it will inspire you to see beyond the obvious when it comes to creating lovely things.

I've designed most of the projects specifically for this book, and I know that they'll get you noticed. The diva in you will be delighted, and shrinking violets will shine.

I hope you enjoy the ride!

the treasure hunt

Looking chic and unique on a shoestring is a challenge, but it's an entirely pleasurable one. Commandeer a sturdy old-fashioned hatbox or a redundant laundry basket and turn it into your secret textile treasure chest. Your mission is to fill it with beautiful finds to transform basic items into sophisticated, elegant and glamorous attire.

Alternatively, you might want to buy a chest of drawers to store all your bits and pieces in. I love old draper's chests and those vintage wooden filing cabinets with dozens of drawers that you can label up in italic handwriting. Of course, if you're really lucky, you might have the space to dedicate an entire cupboard to housing your precious hoard.

Here are some of the things that you should look out for. None of these items will cost you more than a few pounds, and some, considerably less.

Beads – whether they're glass, plastic or wood, beads are great for using as embellishments or working into jewellery. They're easy to sew on. Just make sure you have a needle fine enough to go through the holes of really tiny ones. You can buy special beading needles for this. If you don't want to splash out on new beads, simply re-use the ones you already have.

Buttons – I love buttons and button boxes. I still remember being absorbed for hours sorting through my mother's. She kept her buttons in an old Quality Street chocolate tin, and I'd sit contentedly grouping the multicoloured contents into families. You might already have a button collection of your own. If not, start by putting all those listless spares into a jam jar. Even the plainest ones should have a happy home. Clothes often still come with an extra button, so add them to the jar too. Then look out for particularly pretty ones to enhance the things you're making. Vintage buttons in particular can be really charming and unusual, and lend your clothes a designer twist.

Also worth having to hand are cover buttons for covering in fabrics of your own choice. They're great as a trim. (See Fabric Know-how on page 28.)

Bling – I am a bit of a magpie and love anything that glitters and gleams. Search for sparkly acrylic sew-on gemstones as well as ones with a metallic finish, which give a sophisticated feel and are good for 'toughening up' your look. As I'm always trying to do things quickly and cover surface areas fast, I prefer using larger gems rather than smaller, more fiddly ones. The best place to find these bigger stones is on the internet. Otherwise you can try bead shops and haberdasheries.

Chains – these look great incorporated into jewellery or when customising clothes. You can use pieces of old necklace, or buy them new from haberdasheries. If your

haberdashery or craft shop doesn't stock chain then try DIY stores – they will usually have quite a variety.

Embroidered patches – I'm talking here about embroidered badges or insignia for clothes that you can sew or iron on. I particularly covet those tourist patches, ones that say things like 'I love London'. They look fantastic on hats and bags and evoke memories of journeys, both real and imagined. My latest obsession is old Girl Guide and Scout badges. Sew a few on to a plain jumper to create a cosy retro camping cover-up. Military-style patches, such as sergeant's stripes, suit us style sirens and look the part on jackets and coats.

Fabrics – don't think just of buying fabric by the metre, which can end up being rather expensive. It's much cheaper to cut up clothes you no longer wear, or buy and exchange second-hand clothes for the fabric alone.

Felt – you can buy basic craft felt in squares. You can also purchase thicker felt by the metre. It's useful as a fabric in its own right and for using as a lining or backing material for your accessories.

Feathers – use individual ones to trim hats or to add to jewellery. You can also purchase feathers stitched together by the metre. This trim looks good added to clothing around necklines, shoulders or hems. Do remember though that you can't wash your feather trims so make them removable if you can. If not, you'll have to pay for dry-cleaning, which will be pricey.

Flowers – create your own from fabric

offcuts or look out for fake flowers to sew on to hairslides, hats and other items.

Frogs – oriental-style embellishments, usually made of cord.

Fur – fake fur makes a very luxurious trim on coats, bags and jumpers. Try using it in more unexpected ways too, perhaps along the edge of a skirt, or make little fur pompoms for hats or as a trim for shoes.

Glitter – not just for children!

Hankies – hankies come in lots of beautiful designs. They're already hemmed and are easy to sew together, which makes them perfect for our purposes.

Lace and other pretty haberdashery trims – if you see something you like and it's not expensive then buy it, even if you don't have something in mind for it immediately. It might inspire you. I often spot a beautiful

vintage trim and then look out for a cheap or second-hand cardigan to sew it on to. Don't limit yourself to clothing trims. Upholstery trims are also fantastic for using on clothes and accessories.

Leather and suede – you can get scraps of leather from all sorts of places, and in all kinds of textures and colours. Try shops that make or sell leather clothing, as they often have offcuts going begging. If you're really struggling to find some, then look out for an old leather skirt or trousers to cut up. Just make sure you use the rest of the hide for something creative too.

Old hand-embroidered linen – this includes items such as pillowcases, covers, tablecloths, mats, runners and delicate lace doilies. These items often entailed hours of work and now, rather shamefully, you can pick them up for a song. Give them a new starring role in the things you make. Of course, old linen looks fabulous

used for its original purpose in your home, so be selective. Look out especially for damaged stuff, it's cheaper and less heartbreaking to cut it up. You can always take off the lace edging even if you can't use the fabric itself.

Old jewellery – see Turn-around Trinkets (page 60–1) for more details on what to add to your stash.

Ribbons – build up a selection of eye-catching ribbons to use in your designs. Old-fashioned Petersham ribbon looks lovely and dyes well, so you can buy white and colour it yourself (you can dye small quantities in a pan on the hob). Whether velvet, metallic, satin, spotted, striped or embroidered, ribbons are an inexpensive way of adding a little personality to your clothes. Save ribbons after you've unwrapped presents. Shoelaces are a good thing to have in your collection too, and can be used in unexpected ways.

Sequins – yes please! Again, for me, when it comes to bling, bigger is better. Look out for larger sequins and delicious old vintage ones. You can sometimes find ripped up bits of clothing covered in sequins in scrap baskets.

Silk scarves – I could fill my wardrobe with clothes and accessories made out of these and no doubt dress my home in them too. You'll find them in flea markets and second-hand stores the world over in an array of beautiful colours and patterns, and they often cost next to nothing.

Sparkly sew-on or iron-on motifs – these sequin-embellished trims look great on clothes and accessories and are now widely available.

Studs – a tough-looking alternative to sparkle, studs are an easy way of adding textural interest. They look good in burnished silver, gold and bronze. Just poke them through the fabric and bend back the prongs for instant rock chic.

T-shirts – don't chuck them out. The cotton ones are great for making new things as they don't fray and come in lots of colours and patterns.

Tea-towels – even the most boring of tea towels can be turned into something lovely. Old-fashioned linen ones are particularly worth looking out for as they're of a beautiful heavy quality.

Vintage lace collars – you can find intricate vintage lace collars in markets, antique stores and on eBay, often for very little money. They're a perfect way of refreshing your look in a flash.

Wool – good for turning into trims such as pompoms and tassels. Tapestry wool is useful if you don't want to give houseroom to large quantities, and the colours are lovely. Used balls of wool can often be picked up cheaply in charity shops.

So, now you know what to look out for, where should you search for your treasures? I've mentioned a couple of hunting grounds already, but here are some more ideas.

hunting grounds

Antique shops

Items in these shops can be expensive, especially if the shop is in a smaller town, but you'll sometimes unearth unexpected treasures. It's definitely worth having a browse.

Auctions

Check to see what sales are coming up at your local auction house. Specialist textile sales are often for collectors, but general house clearance sales can turn up the odd bargain. I have friends who bought an old wooden chest stuffed with vintage flags and bunting for virtually nothing at one such auction.

Car boot sales

These are usually advertised in local papers or on the internet. You might have to sift through a lot of dross but you can find real gems at bargain prices. It's best to get there early, and have smaller notes and coins with you as this way you're more likely to get a good price. It's always worth haggling and making an offer. I know it's not exactly chic, but do wear a rucksack to go car-booting. If you end up buying lots, you can then stow everything securely and keep your hands free for rifling through further piles of potential bargains. Also, wear comfortable shoes – you'll be amazed at how little things like this can make a huge difference to your stamina!

Charity shops

There are charity shops on every high street. They're great places to find the basics. You can buy quality jumpers and T-shirts for embellishing for very little and, of course, all the money's going to a good cause. Charity-shop shoes are also excellent for experimenting with, and it's not too crushing if things go wrong. Upmarket areas often have very good stock but it can be correspondingly more expensive.

Clothes recycling depots

It's worth finding out where your local clothes/textile recycling depot is and making an appointment to go and have a look. It's an experience in itself, and really opens up your eyes to the way we waste clothes in the West. You might also find some things there that are worth taking home – you won't have to pay much, that's for sure!

Craft/art shops

I find these shops can be a bit hit-and-miss. You'll usually find the basics in most of them – things like jewellery findings and glitter, for example. If you're a regular customer it's always worth telling shop managers that you'd like them to stock something special. People are often very willing to take up useful suggestions.

Flea markets at home and abroad

There's nothing I like more than spending a Sunday morning rummaging around flea markets, especially on the Continent or in the USA. The atmosphere is usually very relaxed and I love the different characters you encounter. You find some fantastic things and you'll often pay a very reasonable price. I once unearthed a whole box of vintage wooden hat blocks in Paris, and have found incredible trims and trinkets in Berlin, Brussels and New York. Even if you don't buy anything (and more often than not you will) you'll come back full of inspiration.

Take a notebook and pencil with you so you can jot down ideas – look at the vintage trims on old clothes and the colour combinations of patterned fabrics. Have your camera with you too, but always ask the stallholder before you take any photos. Some can be a bit funny about it, which is fair enough really. Make sure you keep your money somewhere safe, as pickpockets do prey on tourists. While on the subject of tourism, if you don't speak the local language but you're with someone who does, get them to bargain on your behalf as locals often get better deals than visitors.

Flea markets are sometimes located a long way from cash machines, so go with enough money, some in smaller denominations, and set yourself a spending limit. It's very easy to get carried away, especially when the sun is shining – I speak from bitter experience! That said, it's always the things I haven't purchased that I regret. I still remember spotting a fifties umbrella at a flea market in Rome. I felt I'd already spent enough money, so I resisted. Three years on and I'm still thinking of that umbrella! Yes, I know, it's terribly shallow.

Even if you don't buy anything (and more often than not you will) you'll come back full of inspiration

Friends and relatives

I've had some of the best things given
to me by kind friends and relatives. Once
they know that you'll really appreciate their
old hankies, broken jewellery or half-used
balls of wool, it's amazing what will appear
on your doorstep. Say thank you by making
them something from this book – it will be
very much appreciated. I've also found
friends to be willing accomplices and
embellishment mules. For instance, while
I was working as a journalist at the BBC,
a producer friend was sent to Delhi for a
few months. I asked her to go on a sequin
search on one of her days off and she
came back to the UK laden with an array of
unique and incredibly cheap dazzlers. She
had a fair few adventures during her forays
on my behalf and each time I look at those
sequins I think of her.

Haberdashery shops at home and abroad

There are two types of haberdashers:
the old-fashioned established ones and
the newer, trendier ones. On the whole,
I have to admit I prefer the former. I used
to live in Lyon in France and regularly
frequented one such shop. It was full of
unusual ribbons and trims. Some were 20
or 30 years old, but there was no 'vintage
spin' put on the goods. You simply paid
a reasonable price and walked out happy.
The shops themselves are often beautiful
in their own right, full of dear little glass
cases and drawers. Sewing shops abroad
are always fascinating, as you'll find
things in them that you won't get at home,
meaning that the clothes you embellish or
the accessories you make will look unique.
There is, of course, a place for trendy

If you see something you like and it's not expensive, then buy it, even if you don't have something in mind for it immediately

new haberdasheries – thank goodness these shops are being revived. The prices, however, can be a little too steep for me.

Hardware shops, at home and abroad

Hardware shops are excellent for things like wire, chains, spray paints, glues and varnishes. While you're in there you might well see something odd that will actually make a fabulous trim. Keep an open mind.

Internet shopping and auction sites

I use the internet all the time to buy the sorts of things that I can't find at home. I live in the UK and I often discover things on American sites that I'd never track down here – enormous sew-on jewels, incredible feathers and extra-long hatpins, for example. Auction sites such as eBay are essential to me. I just type in what I'm looking for and see what pops up. I've bought beautiful vintage beads, bags of Girl Guide badges and a plethora of other lovely items. Be careful though – auctions can get very addictive!

Jumble sales/ garage sales

Rarer than they used to be, jumble sales are what we had before 'vintage' became the buzzword. If you see a jumble sale, then pop along; you might well find lots of cheap goodies. Garage sales often turn up designer items at bargain prices if that's what you're into. You just never know – one person's rubbish will usually be someone else's heart's desire.

Reclamation yards

There's one I go to in Scotland in which I've unearthed the odd treasure. It's by a beach, partly open to the elements, and chock-a-block with everything you can imagine. You have to have a good couple of hours free to rummage, and prices are rather random. They're marvellous places though in which to find pieces of old furniture to keep your textile treasures in.

Skips

I know you're not meant to take things from skips, but I did once find a load of fabulous fabric and wallpaper sample books that someone had chucked. They were far too good to throw away, so I rescued them. Boy, they were heavy! Another friend found an antique wedding dress and matching shoes. You just never know what you might spot, so keep your eyes peeled. Do ask permission before you raid a skip because it's polite and keeps you on the right side of the law. Never trespass – skips on people's driveways are out of bounds unless you check with the owners. And leave the skip tidier than when you found it.

Swaps/exchanges

It's always worth arranging a clothes swap or exchange. It's a good way of offloading things you no longer want and you might come away with something you love.

Vintage fairs

These are sometimes rather pricey, but go along for inspiration if nothing else. Ideas are worth their weight in gold. However, if you're going to buy, you'll find lengths of beautiful lace and trims that you'll struggle

to track down elsewhere. You might also come away with a fabulous dress from the forties – and why not? Surely if you're sensible most of the time you can splash out occasionally? It'll look a million dollars teamed with those beautiful accessories you'll be making.

There's nothing I like more than spending a morning rummaging around a flea market

the basic kit

There are some basic tools and materials that are worth getting hold of if you're going to delve into the wonderful world of sewing and making. Here are the ones I use most often in **Chic on a Shoestring**.

Bodkin

A special type of blunt needle with a large eye useful for threading elastic. You can also use a safety pin to do this by attaching it to one end of the elastic.

Bondaweb

Bondaweb is the brand name for washable and fusible webbing. It's adhesive on both sides (one side is normally covered in paper) and you iron it into place. It's used to stabilise fabrics for craft projects and is a quick and fast alternative to hemming clothes and soft furnishings. It comes in different thicknesses or weights – a standard medium thickness should be fine for the projects in this book. It's also good for adding no-sew decorative flourishes to things. Manufacturer's instructions should always be followed.

Scissors for snipping threads

Chalk

Dressmaker's chalk is useful for putting temporary marks on fabrics. You can also buy 'disappearing pens' to do the same job.

Elastic

Elastic is available in different widths and types, and also comes in lots of colours. It's useful for making quick and simple clothes. When threading elastic, either use a bodkin or attach it to a safety pin. This will give you something to hold on to as you're threading.

Glue

Glue is very useful but you need to use the right type for the job. I find a strong, clear, all-purpose adhesive (such as UHU) works extremely well for most projects that need glue. So unless specified otherwise, use this in the projects. Do not use superglue as a substitute as you'll end up sticking yourself together. If you need to wash whatever you're gluing, buy a washable fabric or beading glue. Different brands of glue work in different ways so always read and follow the manufacturer's instructions.

Chalk

Image transfer paper

This stuff is great fun – and you can use it with a home computer and basic printer. It allows you to transfer images, photos or graphics straight on to fabric, enabling you to personalise your work. You buy it as a pack of A4 fabric sheets. There are a few different manufacturers, so simply follow the instructions for the brand that you buy. It's great being able to sew family snaps or beautiful words on to things like bags, necklaces and even clothes. It's well worth the money.

Iron

A steam iron is essential for pressing fabrics. Use the correct heat setting for the type of material. A damp cloth placed between the iron and the fabric is a good way of preventing iron marks, as well as helping to 'set' folds, pleats, hems, etc.

Iron-on interfacing

This is like Bondaweb but only has one fusible glue-covered side. It's perfect for stabilising fabrics, giving them a bit more solidity, and helps stop them from fraying.

Labels

Mary Jane Millinery
maryjanemillinery.co.uk

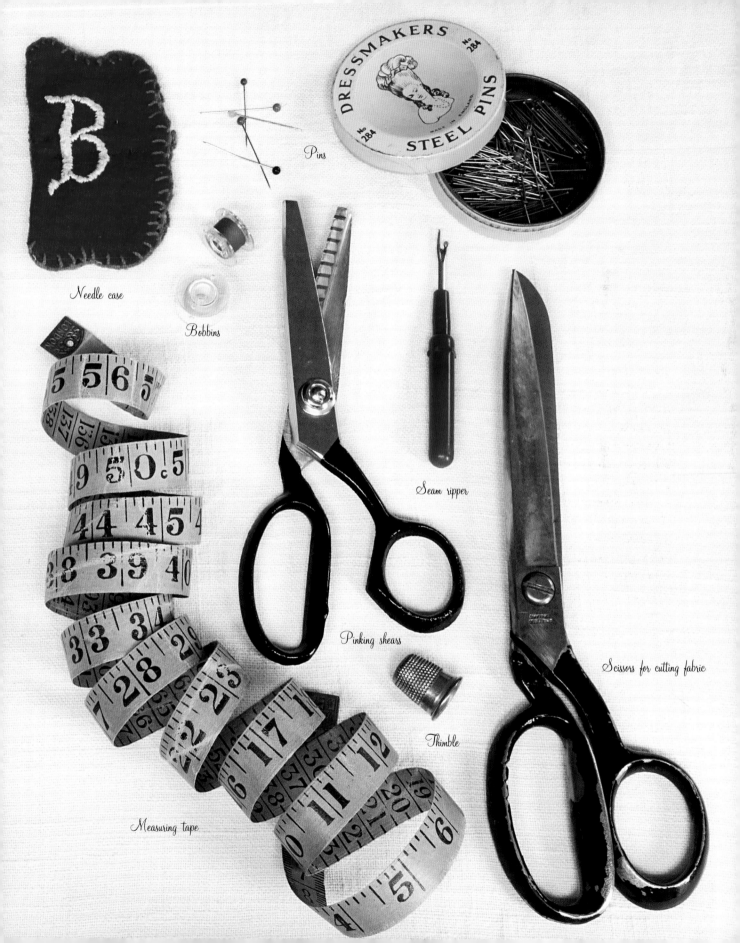

Needle case

Pins

STEEL PINS

DRESSMAKERS

Bobbins

Seam ripper

Pinking shears

Thimble

Scissors for cutting fabric

Measuring tape

Pick a medium thickness or weight and follow the manufacturer's instructions.

Jewellery findings

These are the bits and pieces used for making jewellery and you can find them in most craft stores or on the internet. They only cost a few pence each. I find I mostly use brooch backs (for attaching brooches), shoe clips (for making things clip on to shoes) and the posts, hooks and clips for making earrings. A note on earring posts: try to find larger ones if possible – they're less fiddly and are easier to fix in place.

And just a word on the earring clips: I wear lots of clip-on earrings and I find that the modern clips often pinch my ears, making them quite painful. The old vintage ones are more comfortable as they're bigger, so look out for those. You can sometimes prise them off old earrings – especially useful if you find a batch of odd ones. Re-use the decorative front part for something else. Both old and new clips can be adjusted by changing the amount of tension in the little hinge. Ease the hinge off and adjust the tiny prong before reassembling.

Also very useful are the small metal hoops called 'jump rings', which allow you to attach things like charms to bracelets, necklaces, etc. They come in different colours, sizes and thicknesses.

Labels

You might remember having woven name tapes stitched into your school clothes in case they got lost. Well, why not have a unique label designed for your own special makes? These days you can get them in loads of pretty colours, and of course you can choose what they say – 'Dreamed up by Mary Jane', for example, or 'Made with love'. There are several companies that do small orders and they don't cost a lot. They'll add a professional finish to your designs and, personalised for a friend, they'd be a fabulous gift for a sewing enthusiast.

Measuring tape

Does what it says on the tin. It's a flexible measuring device that's really useful for textile projects. A kit essential.

Needle and thread

Use a needle designed for the job at hand and buy good-quality ones as cheap ones will often snap. Use a good-quality thread too, which should match what you're making if you don't want your stitches to stand out. Of course you might want to sew some things on in a contrasting thread – buttons, for example, look great stitched on in different colours.

Pins

Pins are indispensable and are useful for holding things in place as you work. You can also pin a simple garment together to check the fit. Pins come in different widths, and some have little bobbles on the end. These are useful as you can see them clearly. Don't buy pins that are too thick as they'll damage your fabric.

Pliers

Pliers are essential for making jewellery. You can get specialist jewellery pliers, which are smaller and daintier than regular pliers. You can manage with the larger ones, but jewellery pliers are best suited to the job.

Scissors

A pair of scissors is a necessary tool for all sewing projects. Ideally you should have three pairs: a small pair for snipping

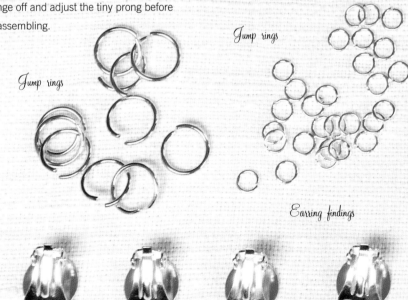

Jump rings

Jump rings

Earring findings

Brooch backs

threads; a larger pair for fabrics; and a pair of zigzag-edged pinking shears, which give a decorative finish and help prevent fraying. Just make sure that whatever you use, it's sharp. Blunt scissors are a real frustration!

Seam ripper

This is a cheap little gadget for ripping apart seams if you mess up. It is particularly useful for taking apart sewing-machine stitches.

Snap fasteners

These are small devices used to fasten two pieces of fabric together. They come in two parts and are perforated with holes so you can sew them on. They're available in different sizes. When sewing them on it's easier and quicker to angle your needle and go through the holes from the side rather than going from bottom to top. Work your way in order around the holes two or three times and finish securely. Remember to sew them on so they click together – it's very easy to put them on the wrong way round!

Safety pin

Thimble

This is a metal or plastic protective covering for the finger – useful for sewing thick fabrics or hides.

Tracing paper

You'll need this to trace the templates from the back of the book. Greaseproof/baking paper is just as good for doing this.

Velcro fastening

Velcro is the brand name for a fabric-type fastening. It consists of two parts. One is covered in

Snap fasteners

hundreds of tiny hooks, and the other in tiny loops. When pressed together they stick. You can buy Velcro in lots of colours and it comes in strips or in little dots that are often self-adhesive. These dots look neater but I've found that they don't always stick as successfully, especially on things like purses that you're opening and closing all the time. There's nothing to stop you sewing these on instead, but it can be a bit fiddly, so try adding a dab of strong adhesive to the dots and see if you can get away with it.

Pierced earring findings

Bodkin

Wire cutters

Please don't use scissors to try and cut wire. Disaster awaits! Use proper wire cutters. Some pliers have a cutting part included in their design.

Headpin findings

Pliers

a sewing phrasebook

In case you need a quick refresher on sewing basics, or want to know what I mean when I talk about certain things in the book, then this section will be a useful reference. It's not a definitive guide to sewing, but just the way I do things. Think of it as a **Chic on a Shoestring** phrasebook.

If you need a more detailed explanation, ask a friend or relative who sews. There are millions out there with the knowledge who are only too willing to share it. Failing that, the internet is a great source of information. These days there are lots of exciting sewing courses and workshops on offer in some very funky places. If you really want to unravel the more intricate mysteries of stitching, then it might be worth finding one that you'd enjoy. Not only will you learn a new skill, but you'll also meet other like-minded people. Before you know it you'll have a new social circle and you'll be passing on your sewing skills to someone else!

Hand-sewing made simple

Beginning

It sounds obvious, but always tie a knot. I'm a fan of chunky knots on the back of your fabric that keep your thread firmly in place. Lick your finger, wrap the thread around it in a tightish loop, roll between thumb and forefinger, and use the nail of your third finger to scrape the thread downwards firmly. It should form a nice knot.

Finishing

People often ask me how to finish their sewing. Here's how I do it: on the wrong side of your fabric, make a couple of small neat stitches one on top of the other, then do another small stitch, but this time bring your needle through the loop of the stitch to make a small knot. Do this twice, then cut off your thread close to the knot.

Single or double thread?

Usually a single thread will suffice, but if you want extra strength, or you're gathering fabric, use a double thread. People sometimes feel happier using a double thread to sew on beads or buttons and it can save time too.

Thread length

I was told never to use a thread longer than my arm, as you can't reach any further. It seems to be good advice.

Six basic hand-sewing stitches

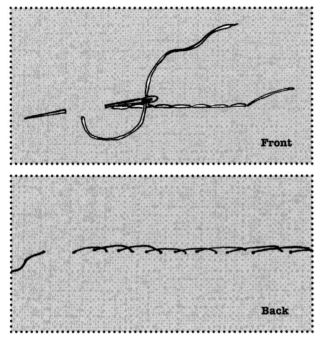

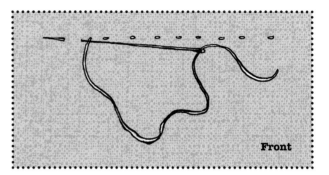

Pinprick stitches

When I talk about pinprick stitches I mean that they should be as tiny as possible. Your needle goes back into the fabric right alongside the little hole it made when coming through it first. Don't worry too much about what it looks like at the back – just make sure the tiny stitches on the front are hardly noticeable. That way your work will look professional to others – no matter how it looks to you.

Backstitch

This is a good strong stitch for holding fabrics together by hand. It is ideal for making clothes. Thread your needle, knot the thread and pull it through the fabric towards you (so the knot will be at the back of whatever you're sewing). Make a stitch of about 5mm so you're back on the side of the knot. Now make a stitch in the opposite direction to your previous stitch of around 1cm. Your needle will come out facing you a stitch length in front of the previous one. Again in the opposite direction to your previous stitch, make another 5mm stitch. Your needle is once again at the back of what you're sewing. Repeat with a 1cm stitch as before, and carry on. You should end up with a continuous overlapping thread on the back of your fabric, and small stitches of 5mm or so facing you.

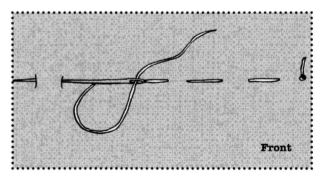

Tacking stitch

This is normally used to hold two pieces of fabric together temporarily. Tie a knot and then sew evenly sized stitches of around 1cm going in the same continuous direction. Finish by doing one stitch on top of the other. Snip through the threads to remove them. It often helps to use a contrasting colour of thread, so you can see which is your tacking thread and which is your proper sewing thread.

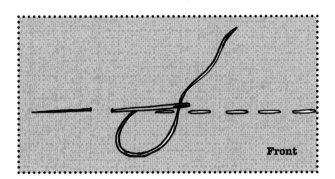

Running stitch

This stitch is simply small stitches that are about 5mm long. It is suitable for gathering up fabric, or just stitching small items together.

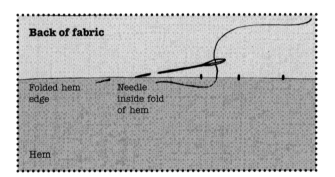

Slip stitch/ invisible hem

This is an ideal stitch to use if you don't want stitches to show on the right side of the fabric. It's often used for hemming. Knot the thread and pull it through so it sits just inside the fold of the hem. Pick up 1mm of fabric on your needle, and come back through to the fold of the hem. Push the needle along this fold and out again a few millimetres along. Don't pull too tight, as you don't want the fabric to pucker. Pick up another 1mm of fabric on your needle and repeat the previous step. The key thing is to keep the stitches on the right side of the fabric as tiny as possible, so they hardly show.

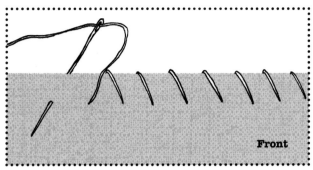

Oversewing

This is used to join two pieces of fabric together right along the edge. Place the edges together and make a small stitch over the top of them, bringing your needle back through towards you a couple of millimetres along. Repeat. Keep the stitches as small as possible if you don't want them to show.

Basic machine-sewing

In this book, the sewing machine is used mainly for speed or for making extra-strong seams. I use a simple straight stitch or a zigzag. Zigzag is good for decorative purposes, or for finishing the edge of fabrics like wool that tend to fray. Zigzag is also useful for stitching together stretchy fabrics. (In this book, I use straight hand stitches for this too as the items concerned are small. As we're not making large-scale garments out of stretchy fabrics it doesn't really make an awful lot of difference.)

When it comes to machine sewing over pins, I think it's much better and far safer to remove them as you sew, otherwise the machine needle can hit them and shatter. Also, some machines don't cope well with lots of bulky fabric so, for example, to stitch the bulky bits on the Bathtowel Cover-up (see page 139) I suggest you revert to hand sewing.

fabric know-how

Cover buttons

1.

2.

3.

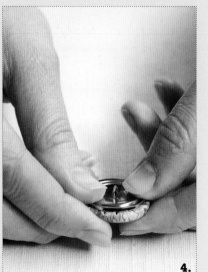

4.

These come in a variety of different sizes. You can cover them in whatever fabric you choose, although very bulky fabrics should be avoided. The buttons are made of metal or plastic and consist of an outer part that you cover and a backing that you click into place.

Cut out a small circle of fabric slightly larger than the button itself (1) and, using a double thread, work a small running stitch around the edge (2). Don't tie off the thread but keep it on your needle. Place the button in the middle and draw up the thread. Do a couple of tiny stitches to secure (3). Trim off any excess fabric and thread. Press the backing into position (4). It will click into place and hold everything together securely.

Finished edge

The finished edge on fabric or clothing is one that looks very neat and doesn't fray. It will have been finished either by hand or machine. It might be the bottom of a jumper for example, or the woven edge of a length of fabric. Silk scarves and hankies come complete with finished edges. You can of course finish edges yourself (see Hemming on page 30).

Fraying

Fraying is what happens to the raw edge of most fabrics if they aren't finished off in some way. Sometimes you might want to encourage it to give accessories a lived-in or rough look. I am definitely a fan. To fray something intentionally, tear the fabric along the grain (see Tearing Fabric on page 30) and then pull any very loose threads away until the fabric seems stable and you are left with a frayed edge. You can trim the frayed bit down to make it neater. Once the fabric has 'settled' it shouldn't fray any further. You may find the occasional thread comes astray in the future – but fear not. Just let it happen and chop it off if need be.

A quick note on woollen jumpers – in this book I use them to make the Cashmere Beanie (see pages 112–14). In theory, if you don't want the raw edges of the cut jumper to fray, you should hem them, or finish them with the sewing machine using a zigzag. However, I've made and worn these hats without hemming many times, and they've been absolutely fine. So I'd save yourself the hassle. It helps minimise fraying if you cut the raw edges with pinking shears. This applies for all fabrics.

Gathering

1.

2.

When you want to gather fabric, lace, etc., use a double thread and tie a knot. Work a running stitch along the edge (1). When you get to the end, leave the needle attached and don't cut off your thread.

Ease the fabric along the thread to gather it up. When you have the sort of gather you want, secure with three or four tiny stitches (2). Finish off as normal.

Sewing on beads or jewels

1.

2.

This is quicker than some people imagine. You don't have to sew on each thing ten times. Just sew through each hole

alternately 2 or 3 times and then move on (1). Sew on jewels 5 or 6 at a time – then if the thread does break they won't all come

off and you can make repairs more easily. Use a single or double thread as you prefer – a heavier jewel may require a double thread, or you may feel more secure always using a double thread. To sew on larger three-dimensional beads, go through the holes alternately (the same as for jewels), but then loop around the threads and bring your needle up through the loop (2). This will keep the threads in the middle tight and prevent the bead from moving around the fabric.

When sewing on embellishments make sure any stitches that might show are as small as possible, and try to use a matching thread. This will help you hide any stray stitches.

Hemming

To make a hem, fold the raw edge of the fabric over on to the wrong side by 2cm (less or more if required) and press with an iron. Then fold the fabric over again by the same amount so the raw edge is tucked away neatly inside. Press again and pin in place, also tacking if required. Finally, secure using invisible hemming or slip stitch or finish neatly with the sewing machine.

Pleating

These are essentially evenly spaced folds that are ironed into the fabric and held in place by stitching.

Pressing

Pressing helps things stay in place and is best done with a steam iron. It's also

useful for opening out seams and adhering Bondaweb. Use a damp cloth between the iron and your fabric if you're worried about getting iron marks on it. Obviously, adjust the temperature of the iron to match the fabric otherwise you'll burn it.

Raw edge

This is the opposite to a finished edge on a piece of fabric or clothing. It is simply cut or torn. Most fabrics will start to fray if left raw, but some fabrics, like T-shirt fabric, will not fray, making them useful and easy to use.

Seam allowance

This is the area between the stitching line and the edge of the material.

Tearing fabric/grain

When you buy fabric you'll often see the salesperson ripping it off the roll rather than cutting it. You'll usually find most fabric will only tear easily one way, along what's called the 'grain'. It will tear automatically in a straight line. You can use this grain to your advantage when tearing off fabric strips to use in your projects. Test the fabric to see which way it will tear. Snip once with a pair of scissors and rip. It should tear easily one way, leaving raw edges that you can then fray neatly or finish in another way.

Wrong side and right side of fabric

The wrong side is the one without the pattern or finish on it. The right side is the one you want people to see and admire.

Sewing on buttons

In this book I use buttons mainly as an embellishment not as a fastening. When using them as an embellishment it's the same method as for attaching beads or jewels. When used as a fastening, you'll need to sew them on even more securely. Stitch 5 or 6 times through the holes, rather than 2 or 3 times, and wrap around the threads just underneath the button a couple of times (1). Stitch through the threads under the button (2), make a loop (3), and pass your thread through it. Do this a couple of times and then snip off the thread just below the button (4). Contrasting threads will make a feature (5).

and finally!

Any journey conducted without planning or a map will very likely mean you get lost and arrive at your destination feeling frazzled. The same is true of these projects. Retain your composure by making sure you read all the instructions for each project before you set out. To help guide you, there are three symbols used throughout the book to show you if a project is Hand-sew, Machine-sew or No-sew. Some are a combination, in which case you will see more than one symbol.

At the end of some projects I've included extra tips to help you get even more out of each idea. So my advice is don't set off until you're thoroughly informed – otherwise you might regret it!

Customising

If you're fairly new to sewing or simply fancy dipping your toe in gently, then try customising and embellishing existing items. With just a few tricks up your sleeve you'll soon be recreating designer looks at high-street prices in only a few minutes.

the ten customising commandments

There's so much stuff out there these days. Many of us have wardrobes crammed with clothes we hardly ever wear. It's pretty wasteful. If I think back to my parents' generation it was a very different situation. They owned far fewer garments and what they had they looked after. 'Sunday best' meant just that. They'd have one 'good' coat or dress that would be relegated to everyday wear only after many months or even years of faithful service. Shoes would be reheeled and resoled time and time again, and hand-me-downs were the norm.

In Britain during the Second World War the availability of materials was vastly reduced. Rationing meant shopping for clothes was a rarity and what was called 'make-do and mend' became a necessity. Clothing was patched, fixed, reworked or jazzed up with unusual trims to give it a longer life. Today, many of us are doing the same thing, for economic reasons and to provide a welcome change to the blandness of the high street.

Try these ten simple suggestions for adding an instant dash of chic. Either hand-sew or use the machine where appropriate, whichever you prefer. Each of The Ten Customising Commandments will take you anything from a few minutes to an hour to complete, depending on how elaborate you want to be. They're ideal for both clothes and accessories.

You're usually safer hand-washing embellished garments unless you've tested your trim in the washing machine first. Certain ribbons will fray and sequins won't stand up to the rigours of a machine-wash.

1. Change the buttons

I've already mentioned that buttons are fabulous to collect and I'm sure that by now you'll have a jar or tin overflowing with some real beauties. So put them to good use and change the buttons on your outfit. See for yourself what a difference it makes.

Here, for example, I've replaced the standard grey plastic buttons on a classic cardigan with fabric-covered ones found at a vintage fair. Immediately this cardie's got something going for it.

This frock has been given a quirky new twist by embellishing it with pink plastic buttons that look like they've come straight from the counter of an old-fashioned sweet shop. They give the dress real personality. So the message is – make the switch and make a statement.

2. Big up the shoulders

Another easy option is to pop in a pair of shoulder pads. Shoulder pads come and go, but there's no doubt that when they're 'in' they can give a real fashion boost to a tired-looking top and add structure to your silhouette.

Buy a pair of small shoulder pads and insert. Stitch them lightly to the shoulder seam to keep them in place. Then add glittery embellishments to the shoulder for added glamour.

3. Take a bow

Tie a little bow from some leftover ribbon, cutting the ends diagonally and stitch in place. It'll only take you a minute, but it will add a sweet, stylish note to your outfit. Sew on a whole row of bows if you want to make this trim work even harder, or use larger ones for more attitude.

4. Lace yourself up

Just add a few centimetres of lace and a couple of well-chosen buttons to change your look completely. Add extra lace to create more of a defined look or trim the edges of a cardigan for ladylike finesse. Sewn on to a T-shirt or any type of top, a vintage lace collar (top left and right) will completely transform it. I've added a little black bow here too, just for extra interest.

5. Go and glitter girl

You can now easily find sequin-embellished trims in haberdashery shops, and you'll certainly have no trouble tracking them down on the internet. Some are iron-on, so you won't have to sew them in place, but even sew-on ones won't take you long to attach.

6. Add some beautiful bobbles

This trim can be bought by the metre, and comes in loads of colours and sizes. It always brings a smile to my face. Sometimes you'll find it in the upholstery section rather than the haberdashery department. Sewn around a neckline it adds an instant hit of colour and fun. Try it around the hem of a skirt, or stitched on to the edges of a scarf. It looks fantastic on umbrellas and certainly makes me sing in the rain!

7. Flower power

Simply attach artificial flowers to your top for a fabulously decadent look. You can sew them on with very few stitches and take them off before washing. For this reason, this trim is probably best suited to wearing for special occasions – you don't want to be adding it and taking it off all the time. Alternatively, sew your flowers on to brooch backs so you can pin in place wherever and whenever you want.

8. Tea for two

I use the lace doilies that used to adorn Grandma's tea tray to great effect in lots of sewing projects. As previously mentioned, you'll often find them in charity shops, as people just don't use them any more. The smaller ones look sweet stitched on to tops with a button or other embellishment in the middle. Just make sure you sew them on in such a way as to keep them flat against the fabric.

9. Riff-raff

This is for fray aficionados. It works particularly well with cotton fabrics and netting. Tear the fabric into a strip of whatever width you want and neatly fray the edges by pulling out the threads until the fraying is even on both sides. Pin in place, pleating as you go, and stitch down, using a small running stitch.

10. Rickrack

Rickrack has been a little neglected, but it's such a wonderful embellishment and reminds me of my childhood. Add on in rows for impact, or simply stitch in place around a collar to highlight a key colour.

Three vintage trims

There's a huge choice of trims out there to experiment with, but sometimes it's fun to make your own. I especially love vintage trims and I'll scour my favourite places for inspiration. When I see something that catches my eye, I'll try to figure out how it was created so that I can have a go myself, which can be cheaper too.

Pompoms

Pompoms are fabulous fripperies that look fantastic used traditionally on winter woollens, and even more striking gracing shoes, bags and jewellery. They have always been popular and during the 'make-do and mend' years they were a cheap and easy way of adding a splash of colour. In short, pompoms equal pleasure and you can now buy them easily in many haberdasheries. However, if you splash out on a few posh pompoms, you'll find your purse is somewhat lighter. Also, you might not find quite the colour you were after.

If you already have some scraps of wool at home, I suggest having a go at making some pompoms yourself. This isn't the laborious method you might remember from your childhood. It's based on the same principle, but will literally take you 10 minutes. By the way, it's handy to have a friend around to help.

You'll need:

- ☐ Cardboard
- ☐ Compass
- ☐ Measuring tape
- ☐ Scissors
- ☐ Wool

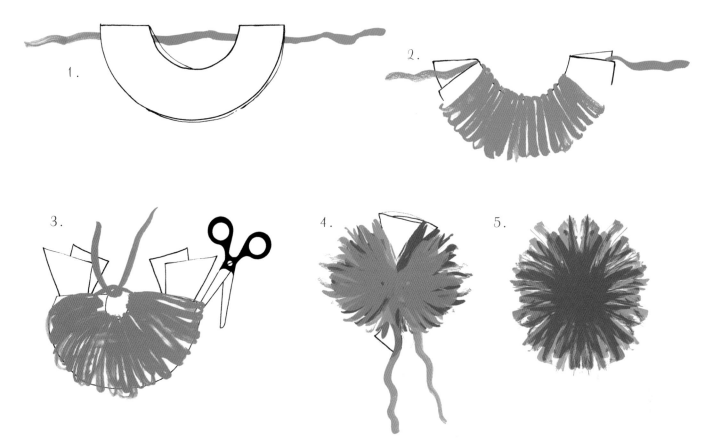

1.

2.

3.

4.

5.

To make pompoms the size featured opposite, cut out just one circle of cardboard (not two as in the traditional method) 4cm across. Fold it in half and cut a curve into it to make the hole in the centre. Place a separate strand of wool about 15cm long inside the fold (1). Now wrap the rest of the wool around the cardboard evenly until it feels like a fat caterpillar. It's important that you don't wrap all the way to the ends of the cardboard, as the wool will fall off. When you've finished, hold the bundle tightly, cut off the wool you've been wrapping with and snip through the ends of the cardboard (2).

Pull the central strand of wool through these snips into the middle and tie once but don't knot. Now, still holding everything very tightly, snip through the wound wool following the curve of the cardboard, taking care that no bits fall out (3). Have a friend on hand to pull together the tied central strand of wool and get them to knot it as tightly as possible (without breaking the wool) at least twice (4). Remove the cardboard.

Fluff out your pompom and trim back any stray bits (5). The more you do it, the easier it will get, and you might even be able to do it without the help of a friend. Cut larger circles of cardboard for larger pompoms.

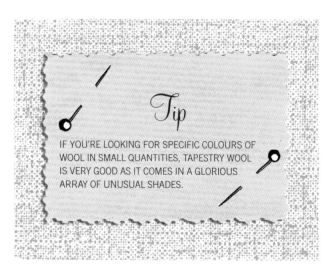

Tip

IF YOU'RE LOOKING FOR SPECIFIC COLOURS OF WOOL IN SMALL QUANTITIES, TAPESTRY WOOL IS VERY GOOD AS IT COMES IN A GLORIOUS ARRAY OF UNUSUAL SHADES.

Tassels

I predict that tassels are about to make a comeback. They are often the runners-up to pompoms in the style stakes, but give those poor tassels a chance. They are even quicker to make than pompoms and can be used to trim all sort of garments and accessories.

You'll need:

- ☐ Cardboard
- ☐ Measuring tape
- ☐ Scissors
- ☐ Wool
- ☐ Sticky tape
- ☐ Large-eyed needle

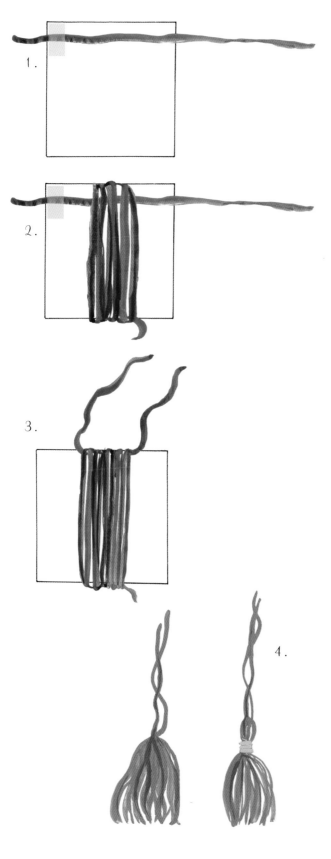

1.

2.

3.

4.

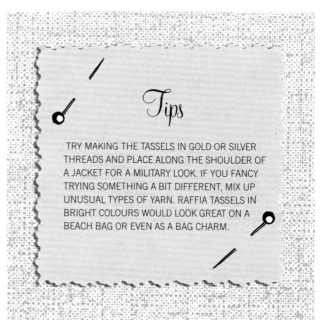

To make a small tassel, cut a square piece of cardboard 6 x 6cm. Place a strand of wool about 15cm in length along one side of the square and keep in place on the edge with a piece of sticky tape (1). Wind the wool around the cardboard and over this lone strand at a 90° angle approximately 6–7 times – wind more for a thicker tassel (2). Cut off the wool at the bottom when you've finished winding. Undo the sticky tape and pull up the strand of wool on both sides (3) and knot. Snip through the bottom ends of the wound wool to free them.

Now finish your tassel by taking another contrasting strand of wool about 50cm long. Leave 1cm free and then start winding it below the head of the tassel about five times and then tie off the ends (4). For a neat finish, thread these loose ends on to a large-eyed needle and pull them through into the upper part of the tassel. Trim to neaten. Make larger tassels by starting out with a larger square of cardboard.

Petersham pleating

I love the vintage look of this trim. I saw it on a little hat from the forties or fifties and figured out how to do it by trial and error. It's a bit tricky, but well worth persevering with. I use it on everything from clothes, to hats, bags and jewellery. If you don't have any Petersham ribbon then you can use normal ribbon, but make sure it's not too slippery.

You'll need:

- ☐ Needle

- ☐ Thread to match ribbon

- ☐ Petersham ribbon (at least 1m long and 2.5cm wide)

- ☐ Scissors

Thread the needle and tie a knot.

Hold the ribbon in front of you. Make a pleat of about 1cm and push the pleat slightly to the side. Hold in place with a pinprick stitch (1). Now put in a second pleat just like the first. It should come halfway up on top of the first, and again be placed slightly to the side (2). Secure with a pinprick stitch.

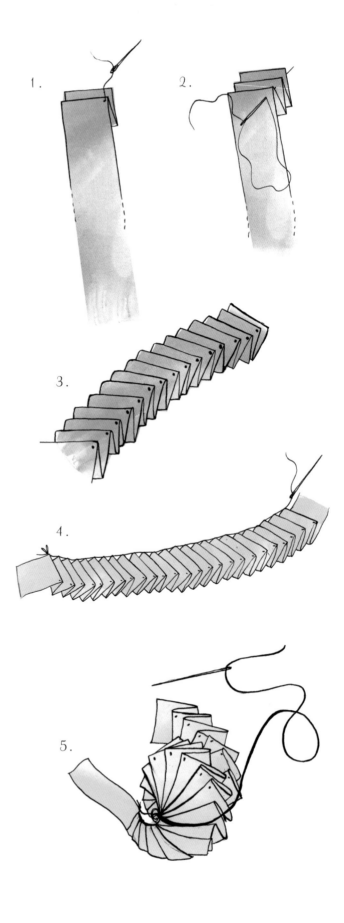

1.

2.

3.

4.

5.

Work your way down the ribbon (3). Your pleats should all be even. On one edge you'll have what looks like a series of little steps, and on the other, a series of little triangles.

Once you've reached the bottom of the ribbon tie off your thread at the back. Now rethread your needle, this time with a double thread, and put a knot at the end.

Pick up the ribbon and, on the opposite edge to your pinprick stitches, catch the tips of the Petersham on your needle (4).

Go down the length of the ribbon. When you get to the end, pull the thread and the ribbon will start to curl (5).

Make the ribbon curl as much as you wish, and hold with a couple of stitches at the back. You can sew this trim on to anything – secure around the outer edge of the curls, at the tips, with pinprick stitches. It will look extremely elegant and very original.

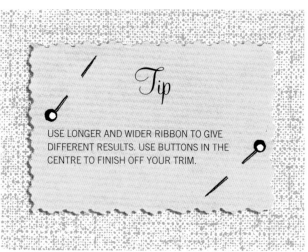

Tip

USE LONGER AND WIDER RIBBON TO GIVE DIFFERENT RESULTS. USE BUTTONS IN THE CENTRE TO FINISH OFF YOUR TRIM.

Naïve no-sew collar and detachable bow

Another really effective way of customising a simple neckline is to add an iron-on trompe l'oeil collar – so-called of course because it gives the impression of a collar, without the function of one. There's no sewing needed here as I've used Bondaweb, which you just iron on. I've also added a removable bow, which you can either hand- or machine-sew. The great thing about this project is its flexibility. You can make the collar out of whatever you please – pretty floral cotton for summer and maybe fake fur for winter. To make both the collar and bow will take you a couple of hours from start to finish.

I make this collar in two halves to make sure I get a perfect fit. If you're feeling bold you can do it in one piece.

For the collar you'll need:
- ☐ Garment to be embellished
- ☐ Pins
- ☐ Measuring tape
- ☐ Tracing paper
- ☐ Pencil
- ☐ Scissors
- ☐ Medium-weight, double sided Bondaweb
- ☐ Iron
- ☐ Smallish piece of fabric (but big enough to make a collar)
- ☐ Cloth, for pressing

For a bow like the one over the page you'll need in addition:
- ☐ More fabric
- ☐ Needle and thread
- ☐ Sewing machine (optional)
- ☐ Knitting needle
- ☐ Vintage buckle
- ☐ Tiny bit of felt
- ☐ Large snap fastener
- ☐ Strong, clear, all-purpose adhesive (optional)

Add a variety of home-sewn or vintage bows for a totally eye-catching look.

Collar:

No-sew

Bow:

Hand-sew

Machine-sew

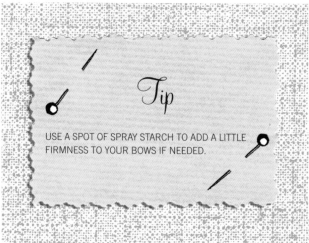

Tip

USE A SPOT OF SPRAY STARCH TO ADD A LITTLE FIRMNESS TO YOUR BOWS IF NEEDED.

First you need to make a collar pattern. Fold the garment in half to find the middle point of the neckline. Mark with a pin and then place the garment flat on the table making sure all the seams are even.

Take the tracing paper and, using the pencil, trace the shape of the neckline from the middle point up to the left or right shoulder seam (1).

Draw half a collar in whatever shape you like. Then copy it, and cut out both pattern pieces. Check the fit against the garment and adjust.

Now pin the pattern pieces to the paper side of the Bondaweb (make sure you have a left and a right). Cut out and iron on to the wrong side of your chosen fabric (2). When cool, cut out carefully.

Peel off the paper and check the fit of the collar against the garment once again (3). Adjust if necessary. Iron the collar into place. Put a damp cloth between the iron and the collar to stop the garment getting iron marks on it.

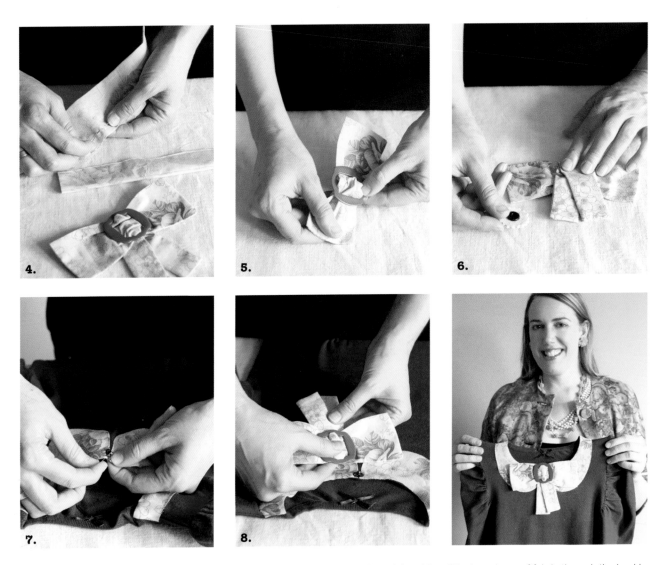

This bow is made in two pieces. Cut out two small rectangles of fabric – the first 18 x 14cm and the second 20 x 8cm. This is just a suggestion of course; you can make your bow any size or shape you like.

Fold each rectangle in half lengthways with the right sides of the fabric together, and either by hand or by using the sewing machine, sew up two sides on each using a 1cm hem allowance (4). Leave the third short side open. Trim back the seams (cutting the corners on the diagonal) and then use a knitting needle to help poke these two tubes the right way out. Press with an iron. Finish the open end on each rectangle by tucking the fabric in on itself. Close using tiny slip stitches. Press once again.

Now thread the wider of the two pieces of fabric through the buckle and arrange neatly in the middle to create a bow (5). Stitch in place on the back, taking care not to let the stitches show on the front. Then fold the second narrower strip of fabric in half widthways and sew to the back of the bow (6).

Cut out a small circle of felt about the size of a two pence piece and sew half of the snap fastener to it. Stick or sew the felt to the back of the buckle and bow. Stitch the other half of the snap fastener to the middle point of the collar (7), then you can attach and detach the bow whenever you fancy (8).

Now have a go at making a different type of bow – just sew half a snap fastener on to the back so you can ring the changes.

Sensational shoe-stoppers

Shoes. Shoes. Shoes! What girl can resist them? They seem to be the ultimate temptation for many women and some would go so far as to say that buying shoes is definitely an addiction. One thing is clear, I've probably wasted more money on shoes that don't fit than on anything else, ever. There were the ridiculously expensive four-inch heels, which instead of allowing me to dance all night as I intended, only managed to get me from the front door to the taxi. Or the strappy sandals which, in spite of being the envy of all my friends, inflicted blisters as big as boiled sweets. So much for twinkle toes!

But surely one can be chic, well shod, in credit and not crippled? What about creating different looks with the same shoe? Then you could cut down on the number of pairs you need, especially when packing to go on holiday.

Well, in an effort to try to streamline the shoe situation, here are some suggestions to help you up the style stakes, clear out the clutter and give you change left over.

Chichi shoes

When I was a teenager growing up in the 1980s, shoe clips were all the rage. They then disappeared, but recently I've seen them re-emerge as a simple, stylish way of making your footwear work twice as hard. If you're going out in the evening after a day at the office but don't want to be bothered with carrying a second pair of shoes, then just clip on these lovelies. Similarly, they're great for taking on holiday to transform a pair of plain pumps. To make these you'll need to get your hands on some shoe-clip findings. You'll be able to order them on the internet if you can't spot them anywhere else. This will take you 10–20 minutes.

No-sew   Hand-sew

You'll need:

- Needle and thread or strong glue

- Fabulous trims – e.g. old sparkly earrings, cute ribbon bows, fake flowers or a ruffle of lace decorated with sequins

- Pair of shoe-clip findings

- Tiny piece of felt (optional)

Simply glue or sew your chosen item on to the shoe clips. Glued-on items like beads or sparkly stones can sometimes snap off rather easily. Try sticking a little piece of felt to the underside of your sparkly trim first to give a little more grip.

If you feel like doing a bit more 'making' then try some pompom party clips using the pompom trims from page 44. You'll need five small pompoms for each shoe. Knot them together in a bunch. Snip off any excess wool and then sew the pompoms on to the shoe clips to create a unique trim. The Petersham pleating (page 48) would look equally good and give a real ladylike elegance to your footwear.

Change your laces

It might seem rather obvious, but changing your laces can totally freshen up the look of your shoes. How about substituting glittery laces in a pair of plimsolls? Or try using ribbons instead. Torn strips of cotton fabric also look cool – the frayed edge gives a hint of nonchalance. Leather laces will toughen up your look in record time. This will only take you about 5 minutes to do.

Embellished plimsolls

Take a pair of plain plimsolls, a clutch of sparkly gems and a needle and thread. In no time at all you'll have transformed your plain Janes into party animals. Studs are also easy to use and are very effective – you just press them through the canvas and fold the little prongs back on themselves to secure. You can also use fabric pens on canvas shoes to give them a makeover. Just follow the manufacturer's instructions. I knocked the newness out of these baseball boots by spraying them first with a little silver and gold spray paint.

Beautiful brogues

This no-sew makeover transforms the look of lace-up shoes completely, giving the impression of a smart pair of brogues. There's no pattern as it depends on the style of your shoes, so follow the instructions carefully to give it a go yourself. It will only take you an hour.

You'll need:

- ◻ Pair of lace-up shoes
- ◻ Tracing paper
- ◻ Pen
- ◻ Sharp scissors
- ◻ Scrap of medium-weight leather or suede (nothing too thick), roughly 40 x 40cm
- ◻ Hole punch (I used a paper punch and it worked – if it doesn't work for you, then you'll need to use a proper leather punch)
- ◻ Strong, clear, all-purpose adhesive

Lace up your shoes and place the tracing paper over the laced-up section. Mark the position of the eyelets on the tracing paper with the pen (1). Draw a shape similar to the one in the illustration around the eyelets, leaving enough room at the bottom to create fringing and enough room at the top for a turnover. This turnover needs to be long enough to extend back on itself beneath the first set of eyelets.

Cut out the pattern (2) and draw around it twice, once for each shoe, on to the reverse side of the leather or suede. Mark the eyelets by pressing the pen through the paper to leave a dot. Cut out the leather or suede and punch in the holes where the dots are. Check against your shoe, then fold back the turnover, so it extends beneath the first set of holes; mark the position with a pen and punch out matching holes here too.

Cut fringing on to the bottom of the leather/suede using very sharp scissors, then lace the leather/suede on to your shoes in your preferred style (3).

To make tassels for the laces, cut two small strips of leather/suede about 4 x 5cm and cut in fringing all the way along the 5cm side, using very sharp scissors. The fringe is roughly two thirds of the width of the leather/suede. Spread the glue on to the inside of the remaining third and roll tightly around your lace. If it's looking too bulky, just trim off any excess. Remember to do this once your laces are in place as you won't be able to lace them up afterwards.

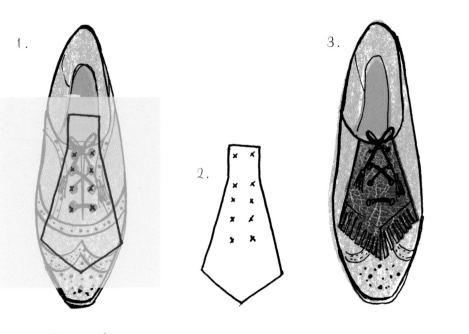

Kitsch-tastic flip-flops

As I write, the kids next door are playing in the paddling pool, the sun is shining and the flowers are blooming. It's a reminder that summer should be about relaxing and having fun. So I make no excuse for the kitsch nature of these flip-flops with their over-the-top floral trim. What's more, this pair is also doing its bit for the environment as each flip-flop is trimmed with a beautiful bloom made from the evil that is plastic bags. These packaging devils do have a teensy bit of an upside though – they make great flowers. It's partly because of the huge variety of colours they come in, and partly because when you manipulate plastic it goes all wavy and crinkly – perfect for giving petals their form. And of course if you flap around in the sea with these flip-flops on, your flowers won't wilt! Chic knows only too well how to do cool, elegant and sophisticated, but it's also grown up enough to let its hair down from time to time. It shouldn't take you more than an hour to embellish these babies.

You'll need:

- Flower template (see page 153)
- Tracing paper
- Pencil
- Pins
- Plastic bags in different colours and designs
- Scissors
- Needle and thread
- Pair of flip-flops
- Bead or jewel for the centre of each flower

Trace the petal template, cut it out and pin it to your plastic bags. Fold the bags up so you can cut several petals out at the same time. You'll need around 12 petals for each flower. Once you've cut the petals out, take each one and tease out the plastic to give the petals some shape. You want them to look wavy and crinkly. Once you've done this, layer the petals up one on top of the other, mixing the colours as you go. Overlap the petals as shown so they don't

all lie exactly the same way. Pin together in the centre and then sew together on the same spot making a cross with your stitches, gently pulling in the plastic as you sew to create more volume. Don't pull too hard or the plastic will rip.

Choose a bright bead or jewel and sew this to the centre of each flower.

Sew your flowers to your flip-flops – they look flattering placed on the outer edge, as shown.

Tips

WHEN SEWING ON THE FLOWERS, STITCH THROUGH THE RUBBER ITSELF AND NOT JUST AROUND IT, OR THEY'LL SLIP DOWN. YOU MIGHT NEED A THIMBLE TO HELP YOU. ATTACH THESE TRIMS TO SHOWER HATS AND UMBRELLAS TOO!

Hand-sew

Turn-around trinkets

If you're anything like me you'll have a box of old, tangled-up jewellery stuffed into the back of the wardrobe, taking up space and doing you no favours in the style department. Likely as not, this hoard will contain bits of jewellery that you've been given but have never really worn, or perhaps necklaces that you've found for a few pence in jumble sales that look like they need rescuing from oblivion. It's a good idea to take a second look at this stash of forgotten sparkly stuff, because often it can be transformed into the sort of jewellery you'd love to wear, give to your friends as presents or even sell for profit. Customising isn't just for clothes!

Turn-around trinkets are exactly what you think they are. You take what you've got, and turn them into something else. Try to keep an open mind, for example, a pair of bejewelled pearl discs might not work on a necklace but would look great as a pair of earrings.

You'll need a pair of small pliers so that you can tease things apart and put them back together again. Also essential is a selection of jewellery findings (see page 22). Particularly useful are the small metal hoops called 'jump rings', which allow you to attach things like charms to a bracelet or necklace. A good jewellery-making glue is a handy addition, as is a drill with a very small drill bit. I use this for making holes in little objects that I want to add to my designs – the sorts of things that you might not immediately think of as 'suitable' for making jewellery. I'm talking about miniature cars, doll's-house furniture, cake decorations, plastic farm animals, dice, Scrabble letters, cracker charms, shells, buttons and chandelier drops. You'll find you can attach some of these objects easily to your jewellery. However, some may need to be drilled so you can insert a jump ring through them. Just make sure you do this safely and with the right equipment or get a professional to help. No necklace is worth a nasty accident.

Here are a few ideas to get you started. All of these projects take under an hour, and some, just minutes.

No-sew

Earrings

You can buy both pierced earring findings and the clip-on variety. They can be attached to almost anything in a flash. Just make sure what you use isn't too heavy – or your ears won't thank you for it.

Creative cufflinks

A great present for the man in your life, or the man you'd like to have in your life! You just need a pair of cufflink findings, and with a spot of specialist jewellery glue you can attach anything to them. Try small vintage bone dice, Scrabble letters, old typewriter keys with his initials on them or beautiful buttons. If you want to make cufflinks to match something in particular (a waistcoat, tie or even your dress), then buy some cover buttons. Cover them in your chosen fabric then stick them to your findings. You'll need to make sure you remove the little shank that sticks out for sewing purposes to leave you with a smooth surface for gluing.

New necklaces and bracelets from old

I once saw a very stylish woman on a train wearing a necklace that had essentially been remade out of lots of different old ones. It was really effective, and I thought I'd try it too. I decided to add various charms to mine to jazz it up even more. As mentioned already, you can use anything for your charms, you just need to make sure you can attach them to the chain using jump rings. Do be aware that some charms are heavier than others, and some have a natural back and front. As you're making your necklace or bracelet, check in the mirror to make sure it's hanging the way you want it to. Adjust the positioning of things if necessary to balance it properly. Use items that have a special significance and build up a piece of jewellery that has a real history to it. Finally, if you want a bracelet or necklace that you can undo rather than one that just slips on, then buy the little fasteners to attach to each end.

estring 38

cay

nted stuff,
seven yards

a game Coloured Padua way
negligee
twenty two yards, ten shillings
a yard, trimmed with 2 dozen
and a half of ermine the same
colour, at eight shillings a dozen.

Lady
in the Dress of the Year 1762.

1762

Straightforward Sews

You've cut your teeth with customising, now try these straightforward sewing projects for both hand and machine. They'll bring a dash of panache to the daily routine!

Tie purse/wallet

Charity shops are full of unloved ties just desperate to be turned into something new. This purse uses basic hand-sewing skills and you should be able to make it in under an hour. Give it a girlie twist, or make it for the man in your life – you know how hard they are to buy for!

Take the tie, measure 33cm straight up from the point and cut across the fabric (1).

Place the tie on the table with the wrong side facing you and the point at the top.

Fold over the raw edge by 1.5cm and then fold over again so the raw edge is hidden. Pin in place (2) and then stitch down using small slip stitches (3), trying not to go through to what will be the finished side of your purse. As the tie is double thickness this shouldn't be too tricky.

Fold this neatened edge upwards about 9–10cm (you need to make enough room to stash your bank or travel card). Pin in place and then sew the side seams down (4). Again try not to let your stitches show.

Peel apart the Velcro and pin one bit on to the front of the purse (5) and then stitch down (6). Fold over the pointed flap, so that you can match up the other piece of Velcro and sew this in place too (7). (It doesn't matter if your stitches go all the way through now, as the decoration on the front of the purse will cover up any mess – hurrah!)

Now for the final flourish. Position your chosen decoration on the front of the purse over any stitches and then sew or stick on neatly (8). Remember that sewing is always stronger than gluing – so do sew your decoration in place if need be (you'll have to sew through the Velcro – but that's fine).

You'll need:

- ☐ Old tie (wide 'kipper' variety works best)
- ☐ Measuring tape
- ☐ Scissors
- ☐ Needle and thread
- ☐ Pins
- ☐ Little piece of Velcro
- ☐ Button or other decoration for front
- ☐ Strong, clear, all-purpose adhesive (optional)

Hand-sew

1.

2.

3.

4.

5.

6.

7.

8.

Tip

TRY MAKING A SLIGHTLY LONGER VERSION TO KEEP YOUR SUNGLASSES IN, OR AN EXTRA-LONG VARIATION TO KEEP KNITTING NEEDLES SAFE AND SOUND.

Button bag remake

Personally, I think it's fantastic that we're being encouraged to use cloth bags. The only downside is that you're probably stuck with a load of cheap cloth bags with logos for various companies or products emblazoned across them. Now I understand that it's a useful advertising tool – but sometimes you don't want to be a walking ad. That's where this remake comes in handy. In a couple of hours you can create something special that you'll want to use every day. It's perfect for beginners, as there's very little sewing involved.

This project was inspired by a fabulous hessian holdall created by Duttons for Buttons, a haberdashery supplier based in the North of England. They've been selling buttons since the early 1900s and have a real passion for them. I feel the same way and am pleased to be able to offer my own take on a button bag.

You'll need:

- ◘ 50cm–1m Bondaweb (depending on the size of the bag)
- ◘ 50cm–1m main fabric
- ◘ Scissors
- ◘ Iron
- ◘ Pinking shears
- ◘ Pencil
- ◘ Tracing paper
- ◘ Heart template (see page 152)
- ◘ Contrasting fabric for heart
- ◘ Pins
- ◘ Cloth, for pressing
- ◘ Mix of beautiful buttons
- ◘ Needle and thread
- ◘ Old cloth bag

1.

2.

Tips

SEW BUTTONS ON IN CONTRASTING THREADS FOR EXTRA COLOUR. MAKE UP YOUR OWN TEMPLATES TO USE INSTEAD OF THE HEART – YOUR INITIALS PERHAPS?

This is how to do one side of your bag. Repeat for the second side. Roughly cut out a piece of fabric and a piece of Bondaweb large enough to cover up the bit of the bag you want to decorate. Using an iron, fuse together on the wrong side of the fabric according to the manufacturer's instructions (1). Now neatly cut the bonded fabric into the shape you want using the pinking shears (2). This gives a lovely decorative edge.

Hand-sew

3.

4.

5.

6.

7.

8.

Trace the heart template on to some tracing paper and cut out. Roughly cut a piece of fabric and a piece of Bondaweb large enough for the heart. Using an iron, fuse together on the wrong side of the fabric. Pin the heart template on to the bonded fabric, and cut out using pinking shears (3).

Now peel the paper off the fabric heart (4) and fuse this into the middle of the main piece of bonded fabric (5). Use a damp cloth between the iron and the fabric, if necessary, to prevent any marks.

Once cool, peel off the paper from the large piece of fabric (6), and then sew your buttons on to the heart (7). Sew on in groups of five or six using a double thread for strength. Try not to overhandle the fabric as you don't want to damage the Bondaweb on the back. It needs to remain intact for when you come to iron it on to the bag.

Once you've finished sewing on the buttons, place the decorative panel on to your bag and iron the whole thing into place (8). Obviously you can't iron over the buttons, but you can iron on the inside of the bag to ensure maximum adhesion. Just make sure your bag isn't lined with plastic first!

Don't worry if the iron-on fabric peels off slightly over time. Just iron it back into place.

'Precious things' drawstring bag

This little bag is perfect for storing your jewellery in, especially when you're travelling. It's equally useful for keeping your hairbrush, make-up or sewing kit in. It's made out of two handkerchiefs and it's as easy as anything to stitch, as your fabric is ready hemmed and neatly square. You can decorate it in whatever way you please. Personalise it with childhood photos or beautiful graphics transferred on to fabric (see image transfer paper on page 20). You can sew this either by hand or machine, or use both. It will take an hour and a half depending on how much you want to sew on in the way of decoration.

You'll need:

- ◻ Two hankies the same size

- ◻ Exciting things to sew on – e.g. scraps of lace, pictures on fabric, buttons, beads

- ◻ Pins

- ◻ Needle and thread

- ◻ Sewing machine (optional)

- ◻ Iron

- ◻ Scissors

- ◻ 1m of thin ribbon

- ◻ Bodkin or safety pin for threading ribbon

Hand-sew   Machine-sew

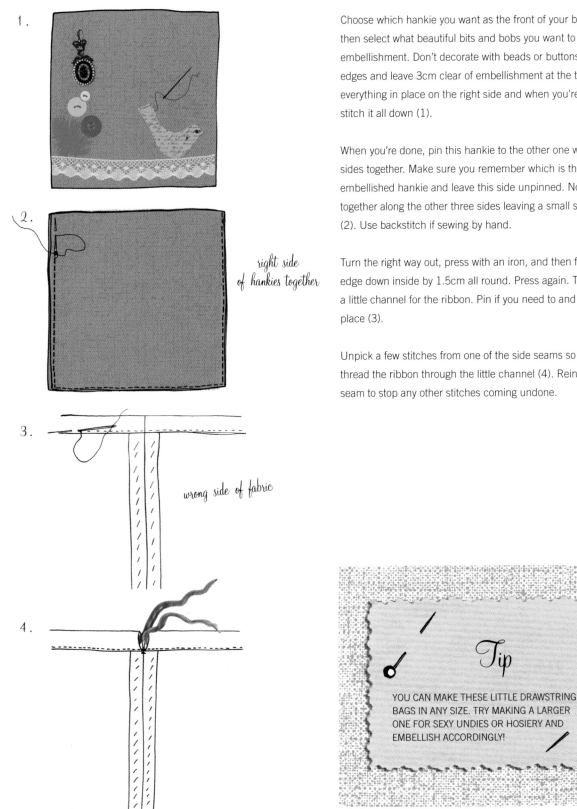

1.

2.

*right side
of hankies together*

3.

wrong side of fabric

4.

Choose which hankie you want as the front of your bag and then select what beautiful bits and bobs you want to sew on as embellishment. Don't decorate with beads or buttons too near the edges and leave 3cm clear of embellishment at the top too. Pin everything in place on the right side and when you're satisfied, stitch it all down (1).

When you're done, pin this hankie to the other one with the right sides together. Make sure you remember which is the top of your embellished hankie and leave this side unpinned. Now stitch together along the other three sides leaving a small seam allowance (2). Use backstitch if sewing by hand.

Turn the right way out, press with an iron, and then fold the top edge down inside by 1.5cm all round. Press again. This will make a little channel for the ribbon. Pin if you need to and then sew in place (3).

Unpick a few stitches from one of the side seams so you can thread the ribbon through the little channel (4). Reinforce this seam to stop any other stitches coming undone.

Tip

YOU CAN MAKE THESE LITTLE DRAWSTRING BAGS IN ANY SIZE. TRY MAKING A LARGER ONE FOR SEXY UNDIES OR HOSIERY AND EMBELLISH ACCORDINGLY!

Tea-towel apron

I remember making an apron and matching oven glove in school at the age of 13 from a piece of old curtain fabric. This duo, which my mother suggested I put into my 'bottom drawer' for future use, must have taken about five weeks! We had to do it all by the letter – cutting out the pattern and pinning and tacking all the pieces in place before ever being allowed near the sewing machine. I'm surprised it didn't stop me sewing altogether. If you have similar memories of interminable school sewing projects then this tea-towel apron with its sweet little frill is for you because you'll complete it quickly with no need for a pattern of any sort. It's cute and practical, and you can make it up as you go along. As well as two tea-towels you'll need an assortment of pretty handkerchiefs and little bits of table linen to make pockets. Use lace doilies and vintage trims for decoration. I've included an old curtain ring in the design so that you can thread through a duster or whatever else you might want to keep at hand. I've wrapped the curtain ring in a scrap of fabric to make it more decorative. Remember, the prettier this apron, the more you'll feel like tackling the housework!

You need an hour and a half to make this apron. I use a sewing machine for speed. You could of course sew everything by hand, but it will take you a while longer. Make sure you wash everything you're going to use to make the apron beforehand so it's all pre-shrunk.

You'll need:

- ◘ Two tea-towels – one for the body of the apron, the other for the frill
- ◘ Measuring tape
- ◘ Scissors
- ◘ Sewing machine
- ◘ Needle and thread
- ◘ Iron
- ◘ Pins
- ◘ Pretty bits and pieces of old table linen, hankies, lace doilies, etc.
- ◘ Large curtain ring and scrap of fabric to wrap around it
- ◘ Ribbon or similar to make apron ties

First you need to make the frill. So, with right sides together, fold one tea-towel in half lengthwise and cut across the length 12cm from the finished edges. You'll then have two strips each 12cm wide and the same length as the tea-towel. Now, keeping the right sides of the fabric facing, make one long strip by machine or hand-sewing one of the 12cm sides together, leaving a 1cm seam allowance (1).

Using an iron, press this strip flat and then thread your needle with a long double thread, knotted at the end. Work a small running stitch down the raw edge of the strip about 1cm in. When you get to the end, pull the fabric along the thread so it starts to frill. You want the frilled strip to be the same length as the bottom edge of the other tea-towel, the one you'll use for the main part of the apron. When the lengths match, secure your thread (2). With right sides together, pin the frill to the main tea-towel, keeping the gathers as even as possible (3). Tack if you wish and then machine in place (4). Finally press the frill down.

Next, arrange your pretty bits and pieces on top of the second tea-towel to see how they'll look as an apron. Hankies and napkins make good pockets, as do other bits of vintage table linen. I like lots of pockets, but it's completely up to you. Once you're happy with your arrangement, pin the pieces in place and stitch them down using a sewing machine. Remove pins as you sew. Strengthen pocket corners by stitching around them twice. Sew circular things in place carefully to stop them from gaping open.

For the cloth-covered curtain ring, wrap it tightly with a narrow strip of fabric. Keep the fabric in place with a few small stitches. Thread the ring through some ribbon to enable you to sew it on easily.

Finally sew your ribbon ties on to the back of the tea-towel. Check you've got enough length to either tie at the back in a bow or alternatively to bring back round again to the front. It depends on how you like it.

Tip

MAKE A GARDENER'S VERSION OUT OF OLD-FASHIONED HEAVY LINEN TEA-TOWELS.

Beautiful belts

Here are some fabulous belt ideas for you to choose from. On the other hand – why choose?
Run up a batch of these beauties. Go for simple and sleek or boho chic. These belts aren't
designed to hold your trousers up – that would be far too pedestrian. Instead they've been
created to cinch in your waist or sit on your hips. I think they look particularly good teamed
with dresses. The first two belts can easily be made by hand in under an hour. I would use
the sewing machine for the Boho Belt as you're piecing various things together. I'd allow an
hour and a half for that one depending on how much you're planning to embellish it.

Ribbon belt

You'll need:

- Two-part belt clip or two-part frogging fixture

- Beautiful ribbon or braid (enough to go around
  your waist with a good few cms extra)

- Pins

- Scissors

- Needle and thread

If you're using a belt clip:

Attach one end of the clip to the ribbon by stitching in place,
turning under the raw edge of the ribbon on the wrong side
to give a neat finish.

Wrap around your waist or hips, depending on where you're going
to wear the belt, and work out where the other end of the clip
should be attached. Finish in the same way.

If you're using a frogging fixture:

Neatly hem one end of the ribbon. Sew on one half of your frogging
fixture, stitching through the cord itself until it's secure. Position the
belt where you're going to wear it and work out the length of the
belt allowing enough for hemming the other end. Attach the second
half of the fixture.

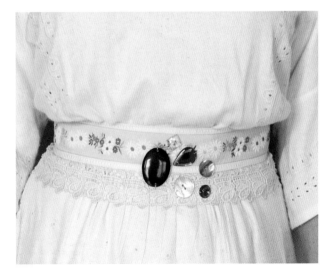

Boho belt

You'll need:

☐ Offcuts of haberdashery and upholstery trimmings – braid, ribbon, lace, buttons, beads, etc. (you'll need some longish pieces – at least 80cm or so – to make the main bit of the belt)

☐ Pins

☐ Sewing machine

☐ Scissors

☐ Needle and thread

Take a longish piece of braid or ribbon to make the central panel. It doesn't have to reach all the way round as you'll add ribbon ties at the end.

It's then a question of playing around with all your bits and pieces to see what you'd like to sew on where. Pin in place and try it on to make sure it's looking gorgeous. When you're happy, stitch things down permanently by machine or hand. Embellish with buttons and other trimmings.

Once you've finished, sew a piece of ribbon to each end of your central panel, ensuring the ribbon is long enough to tie in a bow at the back. Bella!

Tie belt

You'll need:

☐ Tie

☐ Measuring tape

☐ Scissors

☐ Pins

☐ Needle and thread

☐ Buckle (needs to be wide enough for the narrow part of the tie to fit through comfortably)

☐ Two snap fasteners (12mm)

Tip

VINTAGE BUCKLES COME IN GREAT COLOURS AND ARE INEXPENSIVE.

Wrap the tie around your waist or hips depending on where you want to wear the finished belt. You want the narrow part of the tie to overlap the wide part (1). The buckle is purely for show on this belt – it won't really function, as it's the snap fasteners that take the strain.

Work out how much overlap you want and add on an extra 4cm to allow for finishing the raw edge of the narrow part of the belt. Cut off the rest. Hem the edge by folding it back on to the wrong side by 2cm and then by 2cm again so the raw edge is tucked out of sight. Pin and sew in place neatly using slip stitches (2). Make sure your stitches are as small as possible and don't come through to the front of the tie.

Try on again to check for the positioning of the buckle. Mark the position with a pin (3) and sew your buckle in place (4).

Now sew on the snap fasteners. One is positioned underneath the end of the narrow part of the belt and one on top of the wide pointed end (5). Check for fit before you sew all the bits in place – again make sure no stitches show on the front (as the tie is double, this shouldn't be too difficult).

Beautiful Blooms

Here's a profusion of fabric flowers and corsages for you to make by hand. Used singly or in clusters they'll create real impact adorning clothes and accessories.

Best in show rosette

I'm a sucker for an old-fashioned rosette. I love their bright and breezy attitude. Pinned to a homemade card, they make an original easy-to-post birthday gift. I also think these are good for children's parties as kids love making them as well. I've used box-pleated ribbon to give the rosette a slick and professional finish. You can buy it if you want a quick fix or make it yourself (see Tip opposite), if you have the time and inclination. Of course, you don't have to use box-pleated ribbon – you can use a strip of frayed fabric gathered up along one edge instead. It'll just have a different look. I think it's fun to embroider the initials of the recipient on to the front of the rosette, but you could stick some initials on instead or do something else entirely. A rosette should take 45 minutes to an hour depending on whether you're making your own pleated ribbon. These rosettes look lovely on bags and hats too.

You'll need:

- Firm cardboard (e.g. cereal packet)

- Compass

- Scissors

- Approx. 50 x 50cm cotton fabric (depending on size of rosette)

- Pen

- Strong, clear, all-purpose adhesive

- Approx. 50cm box-pleated ribbon (precise amount will depend on size of rosette) or approx. 1m satin ribbon to pleat yourself, plus extra ribbon to make tails

- Brooch-back finding

- Embroidery thread or wool and suitable needle (optional)

- Needle and thread (optional)

(if you make your own ribbon)

Draw two circles the same size on to the card and cut out. One will make the front and one the back of the rosette.

Take your fabric. If you want to embroider any initials on to it, it's easier to do that now, when you have a larger amount to play with.

Centring any initials, place the card circles on the back of the fabric. Draw round them with a pen and cut the fabric out, leaving 1cm extra all round (1).

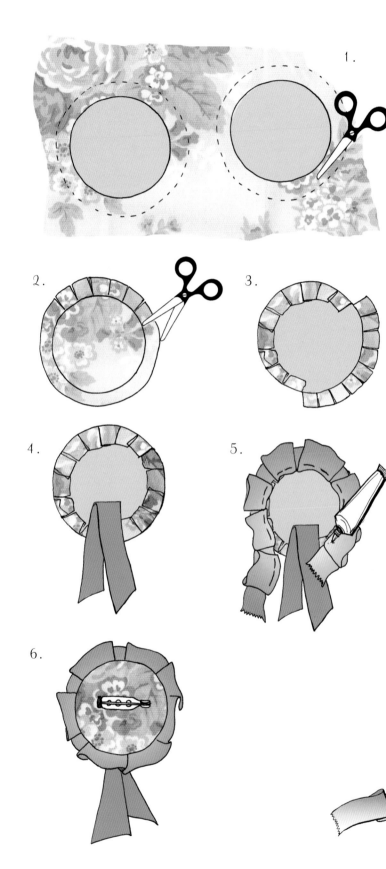

1.

2.

3.

4.

5.

6.

Snip evenly all round the circle, up to the line (2) and place the card circles back in the middle on the reverse side. Put a layer of glue around the edges of the card and fold over the snipped edges neatly (3).

Take what will be the front circle and stick the ribbon tails on to the bottom of the reverse side (4). Now put a thin layer of glue around the edge on the same side and very carefully stick the pleated ribbon in place, hiding any raw edges behind the tails (5). Take care not to get glue everywhere.

Stick or sew a brooch back on to the right side of the second card circle (6), then coat the other side in glue. Press it firmly on to the back of the first circle so that the ribbon is sandwiched in between. You'll now have a lovely rosette.

Tip

TO BOX PLEAT (SEE ILLUSTRATION BELOW), SIMPLY HAND-SEW ONE FORWARD AND ONE BACKWARD PLEAT INTO THE RIBBON, AND WORK YOUR WAY ALONG THE LENGTH, KEEPING THE PLEATS THE SAME SIZE. A COUPLE OF STITCHES ON EACH PLEAT WILL BE ENOUGH TO HOLD THEM IN PLACE. ONCE YOU HAVE THE REQUIRED LENGTH, SIMPLY FINISH OFF AS NORMAL AND CUT THE RIBBON.

Quick and quirky ribbon corsage

This corsage is quick and easy to make. It will brighten up a jacket or dress in an instant. These look great worn in clusters. Make them as cheap and cheerful presents or use them as a lovely decoration on a parcel. Tie one on instead of a bow and the recipient will have an extra gift.

If you want to recycle as well as make something lovely, then use old ribbon you've saved from birthday presents. Alternatively, search your stash for pieces of fabric and rip them into strips so you have a vintage-looking frayed edge. These corsages will take you 20 minutes to make.

You'll need:

- ☐ Four strips of ribbon or fabric approx. 23cm long and max. 3cm wide
- ☐ Pins
- ☐ Needle and thread
- ☐ Scissors
- ☐ Something for the middle – e.g. button or embroidered emblem
- ☐ Strong, clear, all-purpose adhesive
- ☐ Brooch-back finding
- ☐ Small circle of felt

Fold each length of ribbon in half, pin with the ends overlapping a little in the centre (1). Hold together with a couple of stitches, then remove the pin. Place each folded ribbon one on top of the other. Pin them all together and then sew them with a few stitches right through the middle (2). Make sure they're really secure – you don't want them moving about or the ends slipping out.

If you're using a button, sew that into the centre of the ribbons. If you're using an embroidered emblem, you can either sew or stick it on (3).

Sew the brooch back on to the small piece of felt and then stick it to the back of the corsage.

1.

2.

3.

Hand-sew

Sweet and simple fabric flowers

All girlie girls will appreciate these little flowers whether they're grown up or not! They make really pretty brooches or hair accessories and would be a wonderful gift to find in a homemade cracker. They're a great way of using up scraps of cute cotton fabric. I've used a light-weight, iron-on interfacing to give the flowers a little firmness, and it also stops the fabric from fraying. Make sure you adhere the interfacing well by following the manufacturer's instructions.

Use the template to make the flowers. You can enlarge it on a photocopier if you want to play around with the size. You can make a few of these little flowers in an hour or so – even quicker if you get someone to cut out the shapes for you.

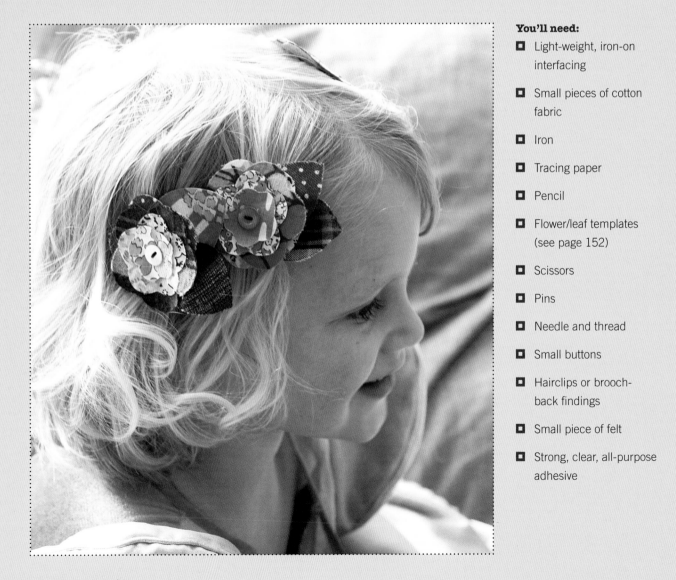

You'll need:

- ☐ Light-weight, iron-on interfacing
- ☐ Small pieces of cotton fabric
- ☐ Iron
- ☐ Tracing paper
- ☐ Pencil
- ☐ Flower/leaf templates (see page 152)
- ☐ Scissors
- ☐ Pins
- ☐ Needle and thread
- ☐ Small buttons
- ☐ Hairclips or brooch-back findings
- ☐ Small piece of felt
- ☐ Strong, clear, all-purpose adhesive

Iron the interfacing on to the back of the pieces of cotton fabric following the manufacturer's instructions.

Trace the templates on to some tracing paper, cut out and pin to the fabric. For each flower you'll need two leaves and four petals: two large, one medium and one small. Save time by cutting out a few of each size at a time. Arrange the petals, using the close-up photograph as a guide, and stitch together in the middle.

Now fold a small pleat into each leaf as indicated on the template. Sew the two leaves together at the bottom edge, placing one on top of the other, at an angle. Stitch them on to the back of the flower right in the middle.

Finally sew a small button on to the front of the flower.

To make a hairclip, cut out a small circle of felt to cover the stitches on the back of the flower. Glue on to the flower and, once dry, glue the whole thing to your hairclip finding.

To make a brooch, sew the brooch finding on to a little circle of felt first, and then stick that to the flower.

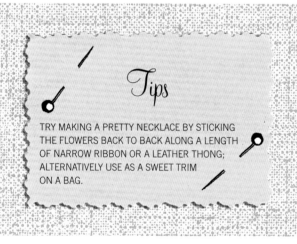

Tips

TRY MAKING A PRETTY NECKLACE BY STICKING THE FLOWERS BACK TO BACK ALONG A LENGTH OF NARROW RIBBON OR A LEATHER THONG; ALTERNATIVELY USE AS A SWEET TRIM ON A BAG.

Hand-sew

Pantyhose petals

Damaged tights and stockings used to be my bête noire. I'd buy a fantastic pair only to wear them once and ladder them. I'd then wonder what on earth I should do, as it seemed like such a waste of money to chuck them away. I started toying with the idea of making flowers out of them, as the variety of colours just seemed perfect for floral creations. Sparkly, patterned or fishnet tights add interest, but tan tights also look very pretty with a little glitter glued into the centre. You'll need stamens to go into the middle of your flowers as well. You can make your own by threading sparkly beads on to fine wire, or you can buy realistic-looking ones from some haberdashers or cookery shops (the stamens are often used for sugarcraft).

You can make a single brooch in half an hour, or make several and wear them clustered together as shown here.

To make a three-petalled flower brooch you'll need:

- ☐ Three bits of stiff wire, each approx. 12cm in length

- ☐ Pliers/wire cutters

- ☐ Strong, clear, all-purpose adhesive

- ☐ Needle and thread

- ☐ Old clean tights

- ☐ Scissors

- ☐ Stamens

- ☐ Small strip of felt or little strip of scrap fabric 1cm wide x 10cm long to cover wire stem

- ☐ Brooch-back finding

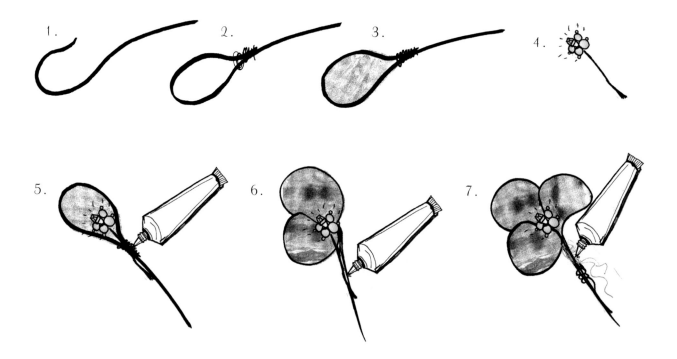

Take one of the lengths of wire and, using pliers or your fingers, bend it into the shape of a shepherd's crook (1). Bring the 'crook' towards the straight side to make a little tennis racket shape. Hold this together by dabbing with glue and then binding with thread (2). Take a small piece of the tights and pull over the 'tennis racket head', gathering together at the join so the tights are really taut. Dab with glue and bind with thread (3). Trim off any excess bits of the tights. Repeat for the other two petals.

Now bend each petal back so the top part curves outwards and it's almost at right angles to the 'stem'. Attach your chosen stamen (4) to the stem of one of the petals by dabbing with glue and binding with thread (5). Then glue and bind each of the other two petals to the first so all three are joined together, with the stamen in the middle (6–7).

Trim back the stem with pliers to 3cm or so. Then wrap the narrow strip of felt or fabric tightly around it, gluing a little as you go to keep it in place and cover up any messiness. Let the glue dry, and then sew your brooch back to the stem through the fabric. Adjust the petals by bending them to suit.

Tips

TRY MAKING BIGGER FLOWERS – JUST START WITH LONGER BITS OF WIRE. YOU CAN ALSO TWIST THE PETALS INTO DIFFERENT SHAPES TO GET DIFFERENT EFFECTS.

NUDE TIGHTS LOOK GOOD WITH GLITTER. JUST SPRITZ A LITTLE SPRAY GLUE ONTO THE FLOWER, SPRINKLE THE GLITTER ON AND SHAKE OFF THE EXCESS.

CLUSTER A FEW FLOWERS TOGETHER (USING A HOT-GLUE GUN) ON A LITTLE SHOP-BOUGHT HAT BASE TO MAKE YOURSELF A STUNNING LITTLE FASCINATOR OR FIX THEM ON TO A HEADBAND. PEOPLE WILL BE AMAZED TO HEAR YOUR FLOWERS ARE MADE OUT OF TIGHTS!

Floribunda

These flowers are great as they're three-dimensional, so they create lots of texture and volume. They're not difficult to make and will look good as a brooch on clothes and accessories. Try experimenting with different types of fabric as you'll get very different results. What about winter tweeds, T-shirt fabric or net? One flower will take you about half an hour to make; you'll get a lot quicker with practice, so you don't have to limit yourself to a three-petal formation, try five or even seven. These flowers look great in clusters, so why not make several and stick them all to one larger piece of backing felt to make a sublime standout floral brooch? Strengthen the backing by sticking on a second layer of felt. Place your brooch back fairly near the top.

You'll need:

- ☐ Compass
- ☐ Scrap paper or card
- ☐ Pins
- ☐ Assortment of fabric
- ☐ Scissors
- ☐ Needle and thread
- ☐ Small piece of felt
- ☐ Button or bead for centre
- ☐ Brooch-back finding
- ☐ Strong clear all-purpose adhesive

Make two circular templates of slightly different sizes. Mine were 11cm and 9cm across. Pin to the fabric. For a basic flower, cut out three fabric circles in each size (1).

Fold each circle in half and do a running stitch along the curved edge, using a double thread with a nice knot at the end. The stitch goes through both layers of fabric (2). Pull up the thread so the fabric puffs, and then secure (3). You've made a petal! Now do the same with all the other circles.

Cut out a small piece of felt slightly larger than a two pence piece. Pin and sew the three large petals on to it (4–5). Then arrange the three smaller petals on top, placing each in a gap. Sew these down too (6). You can then sew a button or bead into the middle (7).

Sew a brooch back to another small piece of felt and then stick this to the reverse of the flower (8).

Hand-sew

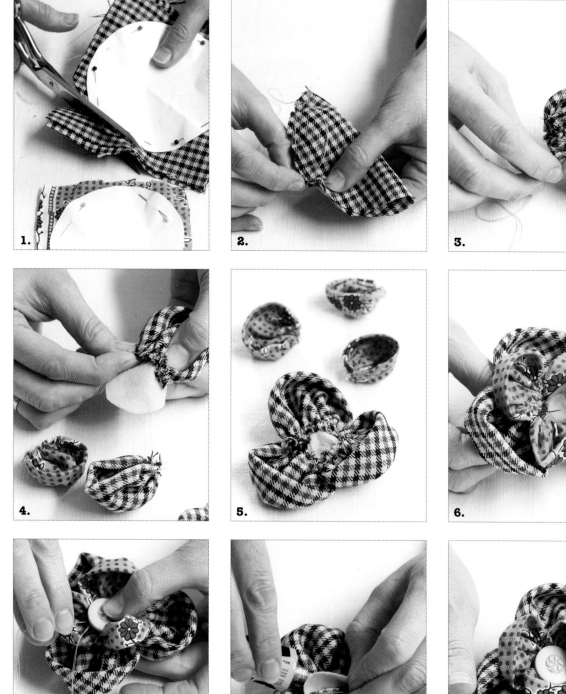

1.

2.

3.

4.

5.

6.

7.

8.

Jewellery

For sheer old-school glamour, audacious design and the frisson of envious glances, look no further than this selection of unique and head-turning pieces, which are stunningly simple to make. You'll be the star of the show!

1950s paste jewellery

Paste jewellery has always really appealed to me. I love the concept. It was first introduced during the eighteenth century when the expense of real diamonds and gemstones fuelled a demand for fakes. Glass was cut (and often foils were added) to create brilliantly refractive stones that could be made into whatever shape your heart desired. Paste jewellery became as sought after as the real thing. Unlike the genuine article though, the fakes weren't limited by size, so designers were free to come up with the most decadent pieces.

Of course, my jewellery isn't paste at all, but the idea of fakery is the same. I've simply sewn sparkly acrylic jewels and sequins on to craft felt. The 1950s tag is there because these pieces remind me of some of the fabulously over-the-top jewels from the period.

There aren't really any instructions as such, the results will be very much down to you. Make up small components first and then incorporate them if you wish into larger ones. Just don't use anything too heavy, especially on your ears.

As mentioned on pages 8–12, you can find sparkling stones and fabulous sequins in all sorts of places. Try to track down unusual vintage ones to create really unique pieces. You can make anything with your sparkling sew-ons: earrings, necklaces, brooches, bracelets, accessories for your hair or clips for your shoes – whatever takes your fancy!

Hand-sew

You'll need:

- ☐ Plastic/acrylic sew-on stones and sequins

- ☐ Needle and thread

- ☐ Craft felt

- ☐ Strong, clear, all-purpose adhesive

- ☐ Small sharp scissors

- ☐ Jewellery findings (optional)

- ☐ Ribbon, to tie on necklaces

Make up individual small clusters of stones and sequins and then sew them on to craft felt, going twice through each hole alternately. Stick another layer of felt to the back and then when dry, cut around the edges of your shapes, taking great care not to snip through any threads.

Use these shapes individually, or group lots together and stick on to more felt to form larger clusters.

To make a stunning necklace use one of the collar templates on pages 154–6 as a base, or design your own and tie on with ribbon sewn to each end.

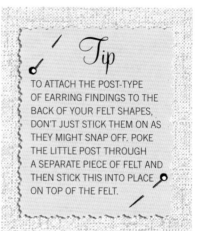

Tip

TO ATTACH THE POST-TYPE OF EARRING FINDINGS TO THE BACK OF YOUR FELT SHAPES, DON'T JUST STICK THEM ON AS THEY MIGHT SNAP OFF. POKE THE LITTLE POST THROUGH A SEPARATE PIECE OF FELT AND THEN STICK THIS INTO PLACE ON TOP OF THE FELT.

Girl-next-door necklace

If you're new to creating your own jewellery, this is chic, cheap and straightforward. Have a go and you'll find yourself with a wonderfully chunky, textured necklace that you can adapt to make very much your own. By lengthening or shortening the fabric strips used, and by mixing up the colours, you'll get different results each time. What's more, the only sewing involved is stitching the fabric to the chain at the end. Easy! Once you've prepared your fabric, you can make this necklace in an hour or so.

Prepare the fabric strips

The fabric strips used in this project are made from torn strips of printed cotton fabric and cut strips of cotton T-shirt fabric. This is to help create lots of contrasting textures.

To prepare the torn strips: take the printed cotton fabric and rip it into strips about 1.5cm wide and at least 60cm long. Fray using the method outlined on page 29.

To prepare the cut strips: cut down the length of the T-shirt. You want strips about 3cm wide. Don't worry about cutting evenly, because when you stretch the strips out the edges will curl to give a perfect finish. You want stretched strips of about 60cm in length.

As I mentioned, you can vary the number, type and length of strips you use, but here's a guide to making a basic necklace.

You'll need:

- ☐ Three strips of torn cotton fabric
- ☐ Five cut and stretched strips of T-shirt fabric
- ☐ Large-eyed bodkin
- ☐ Wooden beads with large holes
- ☐ Scissors
- ☐ Piece of chunky chain (mine was 32cm long)
- ☐ Needle and thread

Randomly tie a knot in the middle of one of your fabric strips and thread the strip on to the bodkin. Then thread on a wooden bead. It will stop at the knot. Tie a knot on the other side of the bead too, so it can't move around. Do this randomly on the other T-shirt and cotton fabric strips, using as many beads as you wish. Make sure you don't place any beads closer than approximately 15cm from the ends of the strips because you'll need to tie them all together at the end.

Now place all the strands on a table and see how they work together. When you're happy, tie the strips together in a large tight knot at either end. Trim back the ends neatly.

Sew on to the chain at either end, making sure you stitch the fabric through the loop of the chain to join the two together.

Hand-sew

Spectacular shoelace necklace

This necklace is amazing, though I say it myself! I took my inspiration from a beautiful dainty little vintage piece; I'm guessing it dated from perhaps the 1920s. I spotted it at a Paris flea market thinking that one day it would inspire me. This is the result. I love the fact that boring shoelaces become something spectacular. Try making a single flower first. You'll have a pretty brooch that you can pin on to clothes or other accessories. Once you're feeling confident, you can make a small choker by sewing three flowers together. Then if you're brave, you can move on to something altogether more ambitious.

Making the flowers is pretty straightforward, the fiddly bit comes in linking them together, which you need to do delicately but firmly with a couple of small stitches where the petals touch. Once you know what you're doing, a single flower will take you about 20 minutes to make, so build up from there.

To make one flower you'll need:

- One flat shoelace at least 95cm long

- Scissors

- Needle and matching thread

- Clear, strong, all-purpose adhesive

- Sequin, button or bead for the centre (don't use anything too heavy)

- Brooch-back finding or narrow ribbon if you're making a necklace

Tips

DYE WHITE SHOELACES IN TEA/ COFFEE FOR A VINTAGE SHADE, OR USE COLOURED LACES. MAKE DIFFERENT-SHAPED FLOWERS WITH DIFFERENT-SIZED PETALS.

Take the shoelace and cut off the taped ends leaving just a tiny bit intact to stop them fraying (1). Thread your needle with a double thread for strength, and have it ready. Make sure you knot the end of the thread.

You're now going to make a 12-petalled flower out of the shoelace. Working from one end of the lace, make a loop of about 7cm and squeeze it flat, so in effect the loop has two sides of 3.5cm each. Secure the loop with a couple of tiny stitches just next to the taped point (2). Repeat the process to create a second loop folded flat on top of the first. Each time you secure a loop, stitch through all the previous loops so they're all linked together (3). Don't pull the thread too tight, you want the petals linked together gently. It helps to keep the petals flat on the table as you work (4). Repeat until you have made 12 petals (5).

Once you've got 12 petals, secure your final stitch and cut off any spare lace, putting a dab of clear glue on the raw edge to prevent it from fraying (6). Let this dry.

Hand-sew

7.

8.

9.

10.

11.

Now pull the petals round to form a circle. Stitch together where the two sides meet (7). Sew a small button or sequin to the centre (8). If you want to make a brooch, then sew on a brooch back to the reverse side now (9).

To make a necklace, create more flowers in the same way. Join together where the petals touch by stitching through them using no knot on the thread (10). Tie off the ends of the thread by hand (11) and cut the thread off very close to the flower (12). Sew a length of ribbon (or half a shoelace) to the middle of the two outside flowers on the reverse side so you can tie on the necklace (13).

12.

13.

Subversive shirt choker

This is unique! The project is so-called because it takes a masculine collar and turns it into something completely feminine. Any 'stuffed shirts' who object to your sartorial style are obviously not worth your association! This is made by hand, but I use a sewing machine to decoratively zigzag around the edges. You can complete this in an hour and a half. There's a certain frayed quality to this piece.

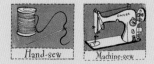

1.

2.

3.

4.

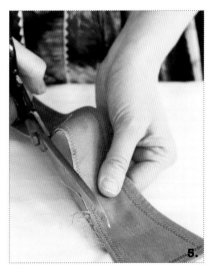

5.

6.

7.

8.

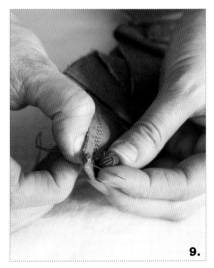

9.

You'll need:

- Man's smart shirt with a stiffish collar
- Scissors
- Iron (make sure it's spotlessly clean)
- Sewing machine
- Measuring tape
- Pins
- Cloth, for pressing (if needed)
- Needle and thread
- Small cute button

Cut the two parts of the collar from the shirt and separate them, cutting as close to the edges as possible, as neatly as you can (1). Give these parts a press (2). You'll notice one side is rumpled and the other more smooth. This smooth side is the one you want facing outwards in all of the following instructions. Keep the rumpled bit on the inside out of view!

Take the lower part of the collar and check for size. It should fit comfortably around your neck with a bit of room to spare (3). You want to wear it with the curved edges sloping downwards. Remove the button. You'll replace it later with a much cuter one!

Using the sewing machine, zigzag right around both parts of the collar, following the shape of the original stitch line closely (4). I think it's fun to do this in a bright contrasting thread. Take care when the machine hits the little plastic bit of stiffening that you often find in collars. Once done, go around the edges with your scissors and trim off any obvious fraying – you're after a neatly frayed look not fraying oblivion! (5)

Take the pointed part of the collar and fold into your required shape using step 6 as a guide. It needs to be around 18cm in length in total. Use pins sparingly to keep the folds in place.

Now place the folded shape on top of the other part of the collar, on the smooth side remember, about 10cm along from where the button was positioned before you removed it (7). The folded shape should be placed so that the smooth non-frayed edge sits below

your chin, the frayed edge pointing downwards. Pin the two pieces together. Check in the mirror, making adjustments if necessary so the choker sits comfortably. When you're happy, press (using a cloth too if needed to prevent any marks) and then sew the two parts together (8). Try to sew between the folds so you won't see the stitches, and where you do see them, make sure you use tiny pinprick stitches. You may need to use a thimble if you find it hard to get through the layers. When you're done, remove any pins and press once again. Replace the original button with a new one that perhaps matches your zigzag stitching (9). Wear the choker with the button at the back.

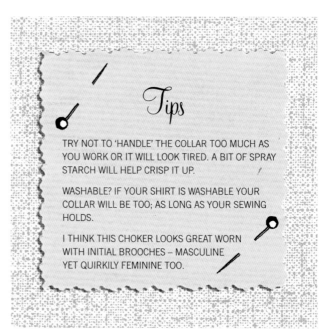

Tips

TRY NOT TO 'HANDLE' THE COLLAR TOO MUCH AS YOU WORK OR IT WILL LOOK TIRED. A BIT OF SPRAY STARCH WILL HELP CRISP IT UP.

WASHABLE? IF YOUR SHIRT IS WASHABLE YOUR COLLAR WILL BE TOO; AS LONG AS YOUR SEWING HOLDS.

I THINK THIS CHOKER LOOKS GREAT WORN WITH INITIAL BROOCHES – MASCULINE YET QUIRKILY FEMININE TOO.

Bella necklace/collar

This beautiful piece can work as either a collar or necklace. It will totally transform a plain outfit, and take you from day to evening in a flash. It uses basic hand-sewing skills and you should be able to complete it in two to three hours, depending on how many things you want to sew on to it. You can use some of the handmade trim and flower ideas from elsewhere in the book. There are two pattern templates on pages 154–6 to choose from, so you can create different looks. You can make the necklaces directly from felt, or use another non-fray fabric. If the fabric is fairly light in weight, it's worth sewing on a felt backing to give it more substance. A backing will also cover up any unruly sewing.

Hand-sew

You'll need:

- ☐ Template (see pages 154–6)
- ☐ Tracing paper
- ☐ Pencil
- ☐ Pins
- ☐ Piece of felt or non-fray fabric for front of necklace
- ☐ Scissors
- ☐ Sequins, sew-on badges, cracker charms, beads, buttons, scraps of lace and ribbon, images transferred on to fabric, brooches, etc.
- ☐ Digital camera
- ☐ Needle and matching thread
- ☐ Length of ribbon
- ☐ Piece of felt the same size as the front for backing

Trace the template of your choice. Pin on to your fabric and cut out.

Start arranging your chosen stash of treasure on to the fabric. Play with different possibilities. If you come up with an arrangement you like, take a couple of photos so that you can remember where everything goes. Don't worry about things being symmetrical or even – this is meant to be random. However, don't put anything too heavy on one side of the necklace without balancing the weight on the other side or your finished piece will slip around when you're wearing it – very annoying.

When you're happy, take everything off of the fabric and stitch it back on bit by bit. It helps to sew on no more than five things at a time so that if you snap a thread, the whole lot won't come undone. Use a double thread for strength. Don't worry about how messy the reverse looks, you can cover that up with the backing.

Once you're happy, try on the necklace and pin in place at the back. Trim down the ends if necessary to get the correct fit. Sew a length of ribbon to each end of the necklace so you can tie it on round your neck. You can wear it either high up or lower down – it's completely up to you!

Take the backing felt and cut out an identical shape to the first one. Trim the edges down so it's a bit smaller all round than the original. Pin to the back of the necklace and sew in place, making sure your stitches don't show up too much on the front. Try to keep them as small as possible. How darling is the finished article?

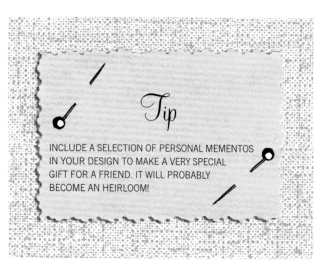

Tip

INCLUDE A SELECTION OF PERSONAL MEMENTOS IN YOUR DESIGN TO MAKE A VERY SPECIAL GIFT FOR A FRIEND. IT WILL PROBABLY BECOME AN HEIRLOOM!

Pompomless earrings

These stunning earrings take their inspiration from the way pompoms are made. They are easy to fashion and cost virtually nothing. You can make them in any colour combination using different types of yarn to get varied effects. By the time you've finished watching your favourite TV show, you'll have made yourself or a friend a couple of pairs. These are for pierced ears, but there's no reason why you can't adapt them and make them clip-on instead.

You'll need:

- ☐ Tracing paper
- ☐ Pencil
- ☐ Cardboard (cereal packet will do fine)
- ☐ Template (see page 153)
- ☐ Scissors
- ☐ Hole punch (optional)
- ☐ Wool or other yarn
- ☐ Large-eyed, blunt darning needle
- ☐ Pair of earring findings (simple wire ones with a little hook will work well)

Trace the template on to some cardboard and cut out. You'll need two circles. The middle is made with a hole punch or just cut it out carefully with small scissors.

With your yarn on the darning needle, thread it through the hole in the cardboard. Start winding the yarn around the doughnut as if you were making a pompom (keep the end of the yarn in place by winding over it a couple of times at the start). When you finish a piece of yarn, just thread the end under a few strands, snip it off and start winding again with a fresh piece of yarn. You can change colours whenever you like. Try to keep your wrapping even, so you don't get any bulges. You'll find at the end, you're really having to push your needle through the doughnut hole, which will get smaller and smaller as you work.

When you're done, thread the end of the yarn under a few strands and snip off. Hook the finished circles to your earring findings and go out for cocktails!

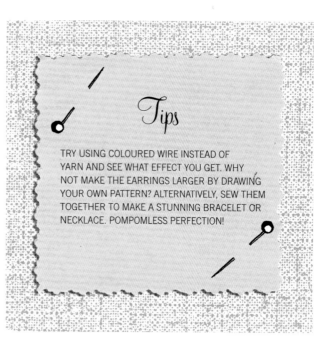

Tips

TRY USING COLOURED WIRE INSTEAD OF YARN AND SEE WHAT EFFECT YOU GET. WHY NOT MAKE THE EARRINGS LARGER BY DRAWING YOUR OWN PATTERN? ALTERNATIVELY, SEW THEM TOGETHER TO MAKE A STUNNING BRACELET OR NECKLACE. POMPOMLESS PERFECTION!

Hand-sew

Glitterball hatpin and earrings

Glitter! Don't you just love it? It takes me straight back to my childhood. These earrings add a little retro sparkle to evenings out. As for the hatpin, well, being a milliner I absolutely had to include a hat accessory in the book. It's so hard to find hatpins nowadays, and when you do, they often consist of nothing more than a couple of beads on a puny stalk. I'm sorry, but that's just not good enough. It's an excuse of a hatpin. Here is a hatpin that knows its important place in the world, one with which to stop the crowds.

To make these you ideally need the cotton/paper balls from craft shops. If you can't find these you can also use polystyrene balls, but be aware that the polystyrene will start to melt on contact with certain solvents and varnishes, so you must use non-solvent PVA glue, and coat very well in glitter before applying varnish or clear adhesive glue otherwise you'll end up with the surface of the moon!

These items are no-sew and will take less than an hour to make, but you might have to add on extra time for drying.

You'll need:

- Cocktail sticks
- Cotton paper balls
- Blu-Tack
- Glitter (mixing the colours adds texture and interest)
- Small bowl or pot
- Basic PVA glue and a brush
- Scrap paper
- Clear nail polish (or spray varnish for larger surfaces)
- Strong, clear, all-purpose adhesive
- Earring/hatpin findings (the hat pin should have a little safety fitting on the end of it)

(If you want to make dangling earrings, make sure you also get the fine wire findings called 'headpin findings' to thread through your Glitterballs, plus a needle to make the hole through the balls too.)

To make the earrings, poke a cocktail stick into the ready-made hole in each of the balls. Put a little mound of Blu-Tack nearby so you can place the balls there to dry. Tip your glitter into a little bowl.

Coat one ball evenly with PVA glue. Hold it above a piece of paper and sprinkle glitter on to it, twisting the cocktail stick round in your fingers as you work. You're building up layers of glitter, not aiming to cover the ball in one go. Secure the cocktail stick in the Blu-Tack while you do the other ball. When the first layer of glitter is dry, put on another layer of glue and sprinkle again with glitter. Do this two or three times until the balls are well covered. Using a sheet of paper means you can tip excess glitter back into the bowl easily.

Once the glitter is completely dry, coat each ball with a layer of clear nail polish. (Twist the balls on the cocktail sticks a little before you apply to make sure they're not stuck on the sticks for good.) Let this dry and then coat with a second layer of polish. The balls should now be well sealed. Ease off the cocktail sticks once dry.

Stick on the earring findings using strong, clear adhesive. If making dangling earrings, poke a needle right through the Glitterball first, then thread the fine wire headpin finding through the hole so you can attach the ball to your earring hook (you'll need small pliers for this). Cover any bare spots on the balls with a further dab of PVA, glitter and varnish.

To make the hatpin, put some strong, clear adhesive on the blunt end of the hatpin finding and stick it up inside the ready-made hole in the ball. Allow it to dry.

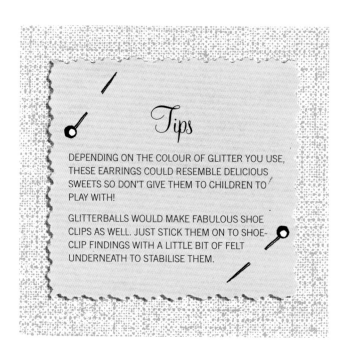

Tips

DEPENDING ON THE COLOUR OF GLITTER YOU USE, THESE EARRINGS COULD RESEMBLE DELICIOUS SWEETS SO DON'T GIVE THEM TO CHILDREN TO PLAY WITH!

GLITTERBALLS WOULD MAKE FABULOUS SHOE CLIPS AS WELL. JUST STICK THEM ON TO SHOE-CLIP FINDINGS WITH A LITTLE BIT OF FELT UNDERNEATH TO STABILISE THEM.

Hats and Headwear

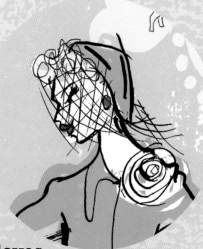

I'm the sort of girl who wishes that hats and gloves were still de rigueur. Of course, being a milliner, I guess I'm bound to think like that. But hats are definitely making a comeback, especially when you broaden out the definition of a hat to headwear in general. From a simple little headband to a full-blown hat, there's something here for every occasion and every level of ability. As for the gloves? Well, I've got those covered too. Take a little look inside.

Cashmere beanie

This is a great way to use up old cashmere jumpers that have either worn out or been attacked by moths. Cashmere makes for a really luxurious and cosy hat. However, if you don't have an old cashmere jumper just use a wool one – a T-shirt will work too. You'll ideally need something with either no ribbing at all along the bottom or no more than 4–5cm of ribbing, otherwise it won't look right. The instructions below will make a lovely slouchy beanie and you can embellish it with whatever catches your eye. You'll almost wish for winter so you can wear it!

The measurements given are for an average-sized head, but they may vary slightly depending on the stretchiness of the fabric. Try on as you're making it to ensure a perfect fit.

You can sew this hat entirely by hand in an hour. You can also use a sewing machine if you want to. Embellishing will take as long as your jewels demand. You might want to finish the edges of your hat if you're worried about fraying. I don't finish mine and it's never been a problem. I do use pinking shears to cut it out though, which I think makes a difference.

You'll need:

- ☐ Old large cashmere or wool jumper (you cut out the hat from the back or front in one piece)

- ☐ Measuring tape

- ☐ Pinking shears

- ☐ Pins

- ☐ Scissors

- ☐ Needle and thread

- ☐ Sewing machine (optional)

- ☐ Embellishments – buttons, baubles, brooches, etc.

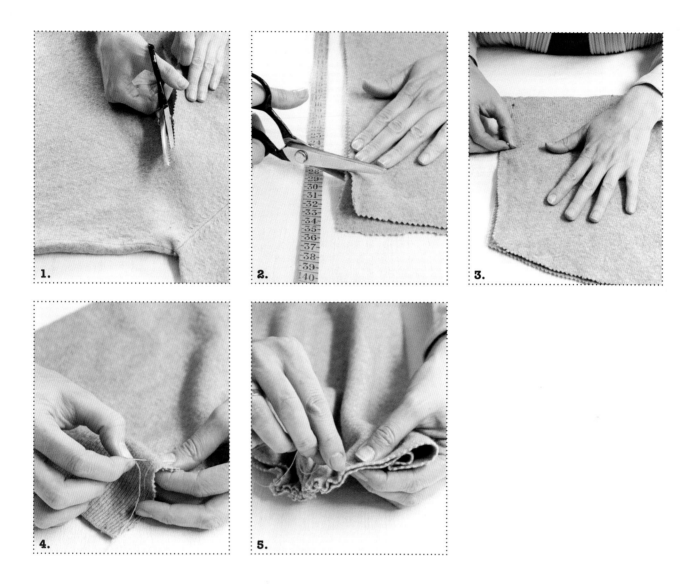

Taking either the front or back of the jumper, measure around 54cm along the bottom edge, then measure up by 33cm to make a rectangle. Cut out using pinking shears (1). Fold the fabric in half with right sides together and place on a table in front of you with the fold on the left-hand side. Trim the opposite side edge so it slopes very slightly down from the top in towards the bottom, making the bottom edge around 52cm.

Now measure 28cm along the raw side edge and cut (using the pinking shears again) in a curve up towards the folded edge (2). Pin the raw side edge and the top curved edge (3) and check for fit on your head, adjusting if necessary.

Either by hand or using the sewing machine, stitch this curved top edge together leaving a 1cm seam allowance. If you're stitching by hand, use double thread and a backstitch for strength. Repeat with the other raw edge (4). Watch those pins don't get caught if you're using the sewing machine!

Thread the needle once more with a double thread and put a big knot at the end. You're now going to gather up the top edge and the raw side edge of the hat, but you'll do it in two stages so you can control the gathering. The folded edge stays as it is.

First the top. Sew a small running stitch along the first line of

6.

7.

8.

stitching (5). Gather up the fabric, and when you're happy with the amount of gather you've got, secure the thread. Repeat this on the other raw side edge, once again following the first line of stitching (6). Turn the hat the right way out (7). Try it on with the gathers to one side. You can always adjust them if you aren't happy.

Embellish the gathering line with whatever you fancy to create a unique winter hat (8).

Tip

YOU CAN MAKE YOUR BEANIE MORE OR LESS SLOUCHY BY SHORTENING THE SIDE MEASUREMENTS WHEN YOU CUT IT OUT. I LIKE MINE LOOSE AND SLOUCHY, AND I FIND IT GETS MORE RELAXED LOOKING THE MORE I WEAR IT.

Fast fingerless gloves or wrist warmers

If you're making the cashmere beanie, then why not have a go at these gloves/wrist warmers too? Having used the body of the jumper for the hat, these beauties give a new lease of life to the sleeves. They're quick, easy and very, very cosy. The look of the gloves will depend on the width of the sleeves themselves. Narrower sleeves will give you a more fitted elegant version, and wider sleeves will be slouchier. Embellish with ribbons, beads, gems, or just keep them simple and sleek. Don't worry if you have a few moth-holes in your sleeves – just cover with gems and no-one need know. Hey presto!

You'll need:

- ☐ Sleeves from a jumper
- ☐ Scissors
- ☐ Pins
- ☐ Needle and matching thread
- ☐ Iron
- ☐ Beads, sequins, etc. for embellishment

Hand-sew

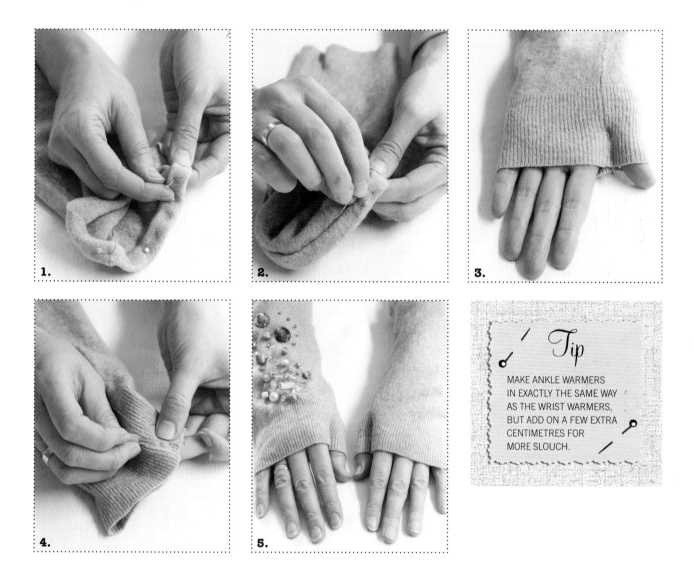

Decide what length you want your gloves or wrist warmers, add on an extra 2cm for hemming, and cut the sleeves from the jumper.

Turn the raw edge over by 1cm and again by another 1cm, so that the raw edge is tucked inside the seam, and pin in place (1). Hem using invisible hemming stitch (2). Press neatly with an iron.

If you're making wrist warmers – you can start embellishing now as you're already done!

To make the fingerless gloves, pull the sleeves on with the non-hemmed edge (ie. the natural wrist of the jumper) half way up your hand. Twist the seam round to lie between your thumb and forefinger on the palm side. Pinch here, and mark with a pin (3).

Using a double thread for strength, sew a 2cm line of little stitches where you've placed the pin (4). Make sure the stitching is really secure by sewing along the same line twice. Finish by tying off the thread inside the glove.

OK – that was simple wasn't it? Now embellish as you wish, sewing on 5 or 6 beads or jewels at a time using a double thread (5).

Tip

MAKE ANKLE WARMERS IN EXACTLY THE SAME WAY AS THE WRIST WARMERS, BUT ADD ON A FEW EXTRA CENTIMETRES FOR MORE SLOUCH.

Emergency hat

There's a moment in every girl's life when she gets an invite out of the blue to a wedding, posh party or other event at which a hat is a must. The ensuing panic about what to wear can be soothed if she knows that she has the ability (rather rare these days) to rustle up a cute little something herself. It's such a handy thing to be able to do and this little pillbox hat should be just the ticket. Imagine your friends' astonishment when you reveal that it's been made from a cereal packet no less. Fortunately, you'll be pleased to hear that the hat is covered in fabric, so should hold up pretty well in inclement weather as long as you don't stray outside for too long in a thunderstorm. It's not too difficult to make and is based on the sorts of methods that professional milliners use, so you can feel very proud of yourself when you've achieved it.

The success of this hat largely depends on using the right type of fabric – nothing too flimsy, but nothing too bulky either. A light-weight wool suiting or robust furnishing cotton will work well, or you could use craft felt. You want something that glue can't seep through. You'll also need to use Copydex glue (the type with a little brush in the lid). Copydex works best in this project when you put a thinnish layer on both sides of whatever it is you're gluing. Allow it to go a little tacky before pressing and holding in place.

Set aside a good couple of hours to make this stunning little hat, and don't rush it. You might find it a little fiddly if you're new to hat-making, but it's worth doing this well. You can decorate your hat with something ready-made, or try one of the other trims in the book.

You'll need:

- ☐ Cardboard (open up a cereal box or use something of a similar weight)

- ☐ Sharp scissors

- ☐ Measuring tape

- ☐ Copydex glue

- ☐ Approximately half metre fabric (as described opposite)

- ☐ Pen/chalk

- ☐ CD (12cm diameter)

- ☐ Needle and thread

- ☐ Pins

- ☐ 50cm round elastic

- ☐ Trim using fabric flowers, a beautiful brooch or whatever else catches your eye

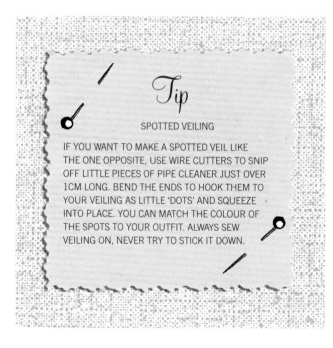

Tip

SPOTTED VEILING

IF YOU WANT TO MAKE A SPOTTED VEIL LIKE THE ONE OPPOSITE, USE WIRE CUTTERS TO SNIP OFF LITTLE PIECES OF PIPE CLEANER JUST OVER 1CM LONG. BEND THE ENDS TO HOOK THEM TO YOUR VEILING AS LITTLE 'DOTS' AND SQUEEZE INTO PLACE. YOU CAN MATCH THE COLOUR OF THE SPOTS TO YOUR OUTFIT. ALWAYS SEW VEILING ON, NEVER TRY TO STICK IT DOWN.

Hand-sew

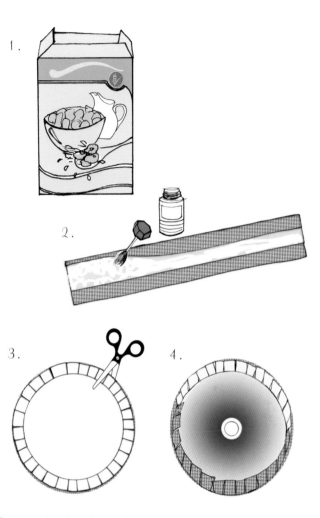

Cut two strips of cardboard. One should be 40 x 4cm, and the other 40 x 3cm. If you're using a cereal box (1), run the strips through your fingers to soften any folds in the cardboard. Glue the card strips to the back of the fabric leaving 1.5cm of fabric spare on each long side. Cut out. Fold this spare fabric over on to the card and glue down (2). Remember to glue both fabric and card. Do the same for both strips of card and leave them to dry.

Draw round the CD on to some card and cut out the circle leaving an extra 1cm all round. Glue this on to the back of the fabric with the circle you've drawn uppermost so you can see it. Allow it to dry thoroughly and cut out.

Snip all round the circle evenly up to the line (3). Place the circle on the table with the right side of the fabric downwards, and put the CD back in the middle. Use this to push against as you fold all the snips upwards (4).

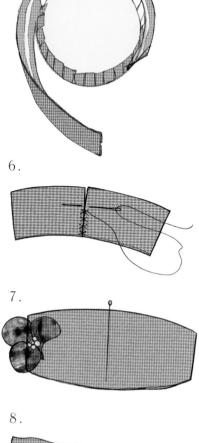

5.

6.

7.

8.

9.

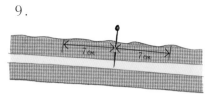

10.

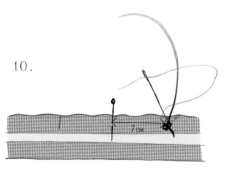

11.

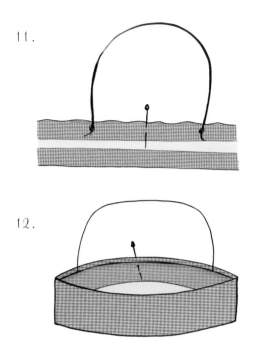

12.

find the middle point of the strip on the slightly fluted side, and mark with a pin. Now measure 7cm on either side of this point (9). Mark each of these points with a little pen mark on the wrong side of the strip. This is where you'll attach the elastic.

Take the elastic and knot one end. Sew it to the wrong side of the strip at one of the 7cm points you've just marked, about 5mm from the edge (10). Stitch it just above the knot and over the elastic so the knot can't slip through. Stitch right through the card. Knot the other end of the elastic and stitch this to the other 7cm point in the same way (11).

Now, with the hat flat on the table, gently pin the lining strip to the inside of the hat (remember, wrong sides facing). Match up the pin marking the front of the hat and the pin marking the middle point of the lining strip. The elastic needs to hang free (12). Try on, adjust the elastic if necessary, and finally glue it all in place.

Cut out a circle of fabric the size of the CD, trim to fit and stick into the hat to complete the lining. Congratulations! You've completed your own couture hat. Remember to wear it with the elastic under your hair, not your chin!

Take out the CD and carefully glue the circle bit by bit to the inside of the larger card strip, pressing firmly as you go (5). It helps to do this with the circular base flat on the table. Take care not to let glue get on your fingers and all over the fabric. Once you get back to the start, trim down the card strip, if necessary, so the sides are flush with each other. Allow to dry and then stitch together, as illustrated (6).

Trim the hat as you please, sticking or sewing any trims in place over the join. Have a look in a mirror and position your hat where you think you'll wear it. Mark the front with a pin (7). The front will probably be a few centimetres to the side of your trim.

Lining and elastic

Take the smaller card strip. It's going to line and strengthen the hat. Gently work your fingers along one of the long edges to pull it out very slightly (8). This will help to ensure a snug fit when you put it inside your hat. Try it for size, with the wrong sides of the strips facing each other, and the slightly fluted edge towards the open end of the hat. The ends of the lining strip will overlap a bit – don't worry about that. You can trim them down later or leave them overlapping if you wish.

Now you've tried it for size, take the smaller strip out again, and

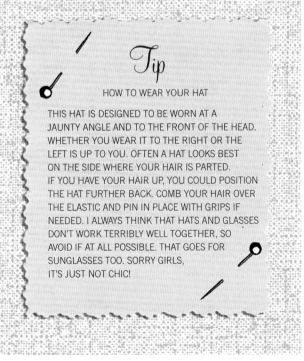

Tip

HOW TO WEAR YOUR HAT

THIS HAT IS DESIGNED TO BE WORN AT A JAUNTY ANGLE AND TO THE FRONT OF THE HEAD. WHETHER YOU WEAR IT TO THE RIGHT OR THE LEFT IS UP TO YOU. OFTEN A HAT LOOKS BEST ON THE SIDE WHERE YOUR HAIR IS PARTED. IF YOU HAVE YOUR HAIR UP, YOU COULD POSITION THE HAT FURTHER BACK. COMB YOUR HAIR OVER THE ELASTIC AND PIN IN PLACE WITH GRIPS IF NEEDED. I ALWAYS THINK THAT HATS AND GLASSES DON'T WORK TERRIBLY WELL TOGETHER, SO AVOID IF AT ALL POSSIBLE. THAT GOES FOR SUNGLASSES TOO. SORRY GIRLS, IT'S JUST NOT CHIC!

Feather fascinator

Feathers are so fabulous. They create instant glamour, and the small feathers from craft shops are relatively cheap. If you want to spend a bit more, peacock and guinea fowl feathers (lovely spots!) are beautiful. When using larger feathers, just use the ends (the pretty end of course, not the other one). If you're a country girl you might know of a friendly farmer or gamekeeper who'll give you some grouse or pheasant feathers for free.

Make up the feather pad to create a beautifully simple hair accessory. Once you know how to make a feather pad you can stick lots of pads together to get an all-over feather effect on a whole hat. You should be able to complete this project in an hour but drying time for the glue must be allowed on top of that.

You'll need:

- ☐ Teardrop template (see page 153)
- ☐ Tracing paper
- ☐ Pencil
- ☐ Pins
- ☐ Craft felt (try to find slightly thicker felt, or stick a couple of layers together if it's very thin. You want enough to cut out two teardrop shapes)
- ☐ Scissors
- ☐ Assortment of feathers
- ☐ Paper bag
- ☐ Strong, clear, all-purpose adhesive
- ☐ Hairclip
- ☐ Needle and thread (optional)
- ☐ One button or other embellishment

No-sew

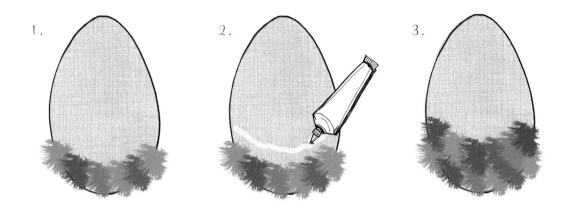

1.　　　　　2.　　　　　3.

Trace the template, pin it on to the felt and cut out two teardrop shapes.

Prepare your feathers by trimming them down to 3–4cm. Remove a few bits of feather from the base of each spine to leave a tiny stalk. Have a paper bag handy for all the discarded bits of feather or else the fluff will fly all over the place.

Stick the feathers row by row on to one of the felt teardrops. Put a thin layer of glue on to the outer rounded edge and press the feathers into place so they overlap the edge of the felt (1). You need the pretty outer edges of the feathers to be free from glue, so make sure you're just sticking down the bottom half of each feather. Make sure the feathers are right side up.

Put another thin layer of glue just above the first row of feathers (2) and stick down the second row so they overlap the first (3).

Continue like this until you reach the end. Rub glue off your hands as you work so it doesn't get everywhere. Let it dry.

Now take the second felt teardrop, cut two little slits into the middle, evenly spaced one above the other, and thread the hairclip through. Cover this pad in glue and stick on to the back of the feather-covered pad. Stick or sew a pretty embellishment to the pointed tip of the pad to cover the last bit of feather. When the whole thing is dry you can clip it into your hair.

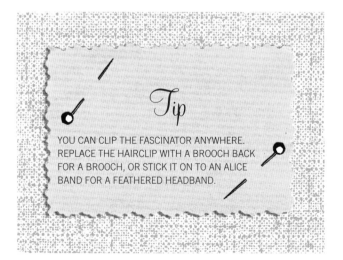

Tip

YOU CAN CLIP THE FASCINATOR ANYWHERE. REPLACE THE HAIRCLIP WITH A BROOCH BACK FOR A BROOCH, OR STICK IT ON TO AN ALICE BAND FOR A FEATHERED HEADBAND.

Retro headband

This handy headband is great for using up scraps of pretty cotton fabric. Each side can be made of different prints, which is fun. I've added a vintage buckle for a bit of extra styling; it gives a slightly sixties feel. If you don't add the buckle the headband will be reversible too. You can whizz these up in under an hour when you get the hang of them.

You'll need:

- Two pieces of fabric 7 x 50cm (cut on the straight grain of the fabric)

- Pins

- Needle and thread (sewing machine optional)

- Knitting needle

- Iron

- Vintage buckle

- Scissors

- Piece of wide elastic 15cm long (longer if you have a large head)

Hand-sew

Machine-sew

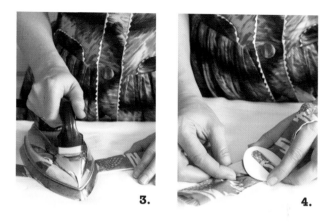

Place the two pieces of fabric with right sides together. Pin and stitch the long sides together either by hand or using the sewing machine with a 1cm seam allowance (1).

Turn the right way out (a knitting needle is helpful here) and you'll have a strip 5cm wide with an opening at each end (2). Press the strip (3). If you're using a vintage buckle, then thread it on now and arrange the fabric neatly to either side of it (4). Leave the buckle unstitched, so you can move it along the headband to different positions.

Turn the openings in on themselves by 1cm or so and slip the piece of elastic into one of the openings by 1cm and pin in place.

Sew the opening down (5). If you're stitching by hand, ensure you go right through the elastic. You don't want your headband pinging off.

Pin the elastic into the second opening and try on for size. You can adjust the length of the elastic here before you sew it down and close the opening (6).

Tip

TRY MAKING THE HEADBANDS IN DIFFERENT WIDTHS, OR SEW DIFFERENT PIECES OF FABRIC TOGETHER IN A STRIP FOR A PATCHWORK EFFECT. HOW ABOUT USING OLD BITS OF EMBROIDERED TABLE LINEN? YOU CAN EMBELLISH THE HEADBANDS TOO OF COURSE, USING BUTTONS, BEADS OR WHATEVER ELSE TAKES YOUR FANCY.

Turban tutorial

During the 1930s and '40s, when women took up so-called men's work for the first time, there was a fashion revolution – namely, women wearing the trousers in the factory and the fields. Now I have to hand it to these girls, because personally I've always struggled with looking chic while turning over clods of earth, but in all those black and white photos there hardly seems a hair out of place. Those go-getting gals still wanted to look glam while giving it some welly, so they adopted the turban, which kept their luscious locks in check.

Now, tying your own turban is a bit of an art, so for many modern-day misses a pull-on turban is a way of getting a dash of forties chic on-the-go. This simple stylish number is made from an old T-shirt. As previously mentioned, T-shirt fabric doesn't fray, so you don't have to worry about finishing the edges. These measurements are for an average-sized head, but they may vary slightly depending on the stretchiness of the fabric. Try on as you're making it to ensure a perfect fit. You can machine-stitch this or sew it by hand in an hour or so.

You'll need:

- ☒ Old large T-shirt (the turban is cut out in one piece from either front or back), plus a piece of contrasting fabric 20 x 10cm

- ☒ Measuring tape

- ☒ Scissors

- ☒ Chalk

- ☒ Pins

- ☒ Needle and thread

- ☒ Sewing machine (optional)

- ☒ Iron

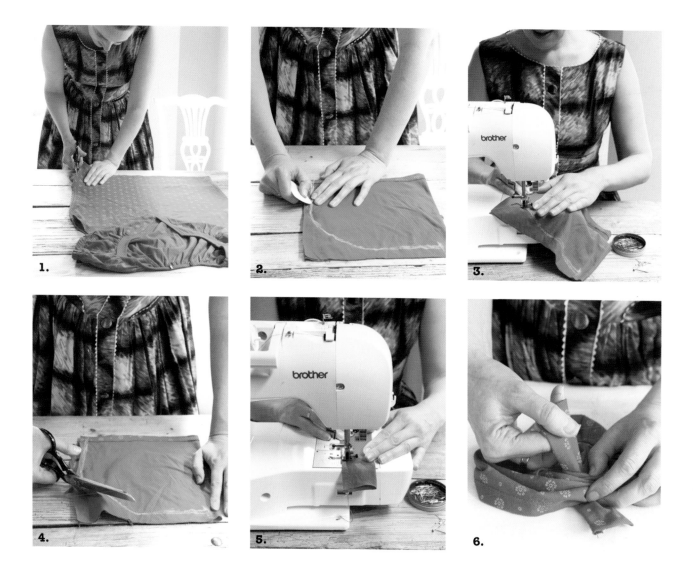

Take either the front or back of the T-shirt. Measure approximately 52cm along the bottom edge, then measure up by 23cm to make a rectangle, and cut out (1). Fold the fabric in half with right sides together, so the bottom edge will now measure 26cm. Place the fabric in front of you with the fold on the left-hand side.

Leaving a little gap of about 2cm at the top (measure 2cm in from the folded edge), use the chalk to draw a curved line down from the top left-hand corner to the bottom right-hand corner of the fabric (2).

Pin along the line, try on, and check for size. Now sew along the line using a backstitch – remember not to sew the 2cm gap! If

you're using a sewing machine, it's best to use a zigzag stitch (3). Be careful not to let the pins get caught in the machine as you sew. Trim off the excess fabric leaving a small seam allowance (4). Press the seams open and turn the turban the right way out.

Cut a small rectangle from the remaining T-shirt fabric, approximately 10 x 14cm in size. Fold this in half with right sides together so you have a tube 5cm wide and 14cm long. Stitch down the long side about 1cm in from the edge (5). Turn the right way out and press this tube flat into a strip.

Thread this strip through the little gap you left at the front of the turban and create a loop, catching all the fabric along the straight

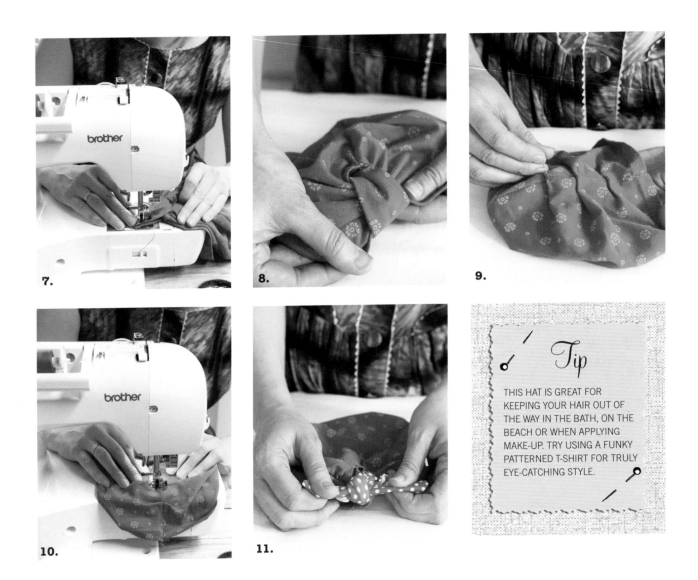

7.

8.

9.

10.

11.

Tip

THIS HAT IS GREAT FOR
KEEPING YOUR HAIR OUT OF
THE WAY IN THE BATH, ON THE
BEACH OR WHEN APPLYING
MAKE-UP. TRY USING A FUNKY
PATTERNED T-SHIRT FOR TRULY
EYE-CATCHING STYLE.

edge of the turban inside it (6). Sew the short edges of the loop together about 1cm from the end (7). Twist round to the back so the seam is hidden (8). Arrange the fabric neatly and close the gap with a couple of stitches if need be. That's the front of the turban finished.

Now you need to put three pleats into the back of the turban to make it fit properly. Hold the turban right side out with the seam in your hand, and fold your first pleat into the fabric about 3cm from the bottom edge. Each pleat should be about 1.5cm deep. Pin the pleat down and repeat twice more until you have three evenly

spaced pleats (9). They should finish just below where the curve begins. Machine-sew (this time using a straight stitch) or hand stitch along the seam line to hold the pleats in place (10). Do this a couple of times to make the seam strong.

Finally, to make the contrast tie for the front of the turban, fold the piece of contrast fabric in half lengthways with right sides together. Sew up the long side with a running stitch or on the machine – leaving a 1cm seam allowance. Turn this tube the right way out and thread it through the loop on the front of the turban, tying in place (11). Cut the ends on the diagonal.

Suitcase Essentials

I thought it would be fun to include a small selection of 'oh-sew-simple' clothes perfect for weekends away. You don't need patterns for these. If you've not made your own clothes from scratch before, then start with these stylish separates and you'll soon be converted. If you're a sewing expert they should take you no time at all.

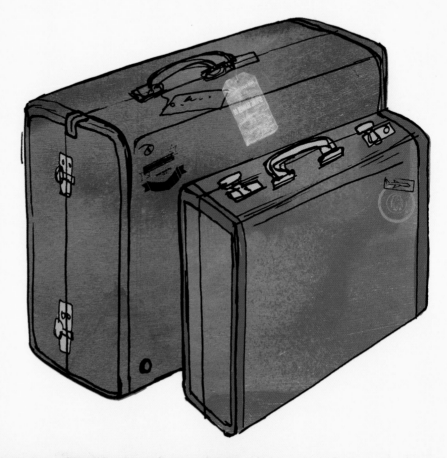

Silk-scarf tops

Square silk or polyester scarves are a fabulous resource. The variety of colours and patterns they come in is truly inspiring. From rich, old-fashioned florals to bright geometrics to quirky souvenir graphics, they offer incredible value for money and have lots of potential. They can be worn in dozens of ways just as they are, adding a shot of colour to a classic coat or blouse. Alternatively, you can add tongue-in-cheek, retro-style glamour by sporting one folded diagonally and knotted under the chin in the manner of Queen Elizabeth II, or alternatively tie yourself an instant turban.

It's a shame that in spite of their versatility scarves often get neglected and end up hanging forlornly on dressing-table mirrors, never getting to go to the ball. So if you want to make more of them, especially the most beautiful ones, then I suggest turning them into clothes. If you're lucky enough to find scarves made of 100 per cent silk it means you're creating expensive clothing for very little cash and it feels wonderful next to the skin too.

You can fold scarves up into the smallest of spaces, making these silk-scarf separates ideal for packing, especially if you're carrying hand luggage only. Slipped on to a hanger and left to unfold in the steam of your bath or shower they won't even need ironing. This is chichi holiday chic on a shoestring!

Just a note on size. The size of the scarves you use for the tops really depends on your dress size, so you might want to experiment a bit. I'm a UK 12–14 and I find that scarves around 65 x 65cm are just right for me. You'll find too that few scarves, especially the older ones, are perfectly square, but if they're out by a couple of centimetres or so it shouldn't really make too much difference. You can always trim down one you really love if it's too big, or sew a couple together if they're too small. Besides, these tops are so simple that you can pin them up first to check the fit before sewing.

Hand-sew   Machine-sew

Sexy summer top
30 minutes

You'll need:

- ☐ 1.5m of ribbon – at least 3cm wide

- ☐ Needle and thread

- ☐ One square scarf (see note opposite on size)

- ☐ Scissors

Cut the ribbon in half and sew one piece to the bottom right-hand corner of your scarf and one to the bottom left-hand corner (sew the ribbon on to the wrong side of the scarf). Tie the other two corners of the scarf around your neck and then wrap the ribbons around your back, around your waist and tie them off at the front over the scarf. That's all there is to it. Go sizzle! This top is perfect for parties and sexy summer evenings after sundown.

Tip

IF THIS TOP IS A LITTLE DARING FOR YOU ON ITS OWN, POP A T-SHIRT OR VEST UNDERNEATH.

1.

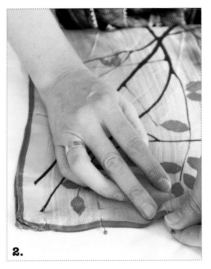

2.

3.

4.

5.

6.

7.

8.

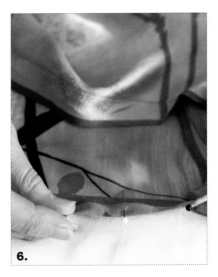

9.

Easy slouchy top

1 hour

You'll need:

- ☐ Two square scarves (see introduction, page 132, for size)
- ☐ Chalk
- ☐ Pins
- ☐ Needle and thread (or use a sewing machine for speed)
- ☐ Scissors
- ☐ Measuring tape
- ☐ Iron
- ☐ 2m narrow ribbon (optional)
- ☐ Safety pin or bodkin (optional)

Look at your scarves to see which way the patterns work (1). Mark the top edges with chalk so you know the top from the bottom.

With right sides facing, pin the scarves together along the top edge (2). Sew these edges together with a 5mm seam allowance (3), leaving a gap in the middle for your head of about 30cm (depending on the size of your head of course!). Measure carefully so the 'shoulders' are the same length. Watch for pins if you're using the sewing machine.

To make the armholes, measure 28cm down from the top of each shoulder (4). Put in a pin, and continue pinning along each of the sides to the bottom. Sew each of the side seams together (5), again leaving about a 5mm seam allowance.

You now have a finished top. Press the seams open, turn the top the right way out and slip it over you head. It looks great belted or simply loose, and you can change the look by wearing the back as the front if you've used two different scarves.

If you want to go one step further and add a drawstring to your top, then you'll need to create a channel to thread the ribbon through. Turn the top inside out and pin up the bottom edge by 2cm all the

way around (6). Press this with an iron, and then sew the top edge down all the way round.

Turn the top the right way out again and unpick a few stitches at the bottom of one of the side seams (7) so you have a little hole through which to thread the ribbon. Attach one end of the ribbon to a safety pin or bodkin (8) to enable you to thread it through the channel (9). Reinforce the side seam with a few extra stitches. Voila! A floaty summer top.

Silk-scarf skirt

There's no end to the uses for silk scarves. This is a very simple, easy-going summery skirt made from two silk scarves. The fact that it feels silky makes it a delight to wear and, like the tops (see pages 132–5), it takes up no room at all in your suitcase. The skirt's personality will depend on the scarves. I decided to use two vintage scarves depicting scenes of Paris, as it fitted in with my travel theme, but you can use whatever pattern or design you want.

The scarves I found for this skirt were roughly 70 x 70cm each. I'm a UK size 12–14, but it could easily fit someone larger or smaller. The skirt has an elasticated waist so it's very adaptable. Don't worry if the scarves aren't the same size, or not exactly square. However, when you sew them together make sure the bottom edges are even all the way round. You can trim excess fabric off the top or simply fold it over when you come to make the channel for the elastic. This is what I'd do too if I wanted to make the skirt shorter. Don't mess with the bottom edge – it's been neatly finished for you, so why make extra work for yourself? You can leave it as it is or add a trimming as I have.

I made this skirt on the sewing machine for speed, and completed it in an hour.

You'll need:

- ☐ Two large silk scarves (see note above on size)

- ☐ Pins

- ☐ Chalk (or safety pin to mark the top of the skirt)

- ☐ Sewing machine

- ☐ Measuring tape

- ☐ Scissors

- ☐ Iron

- ☐ Needle and thread

- ☐ Wide elastic (enough to fit comfortably around your waist leaving 2–3cm of overlap)

- ☐ Safety pin or large bodkin

- ☐ Trim for bottom edge of skirt (optional)

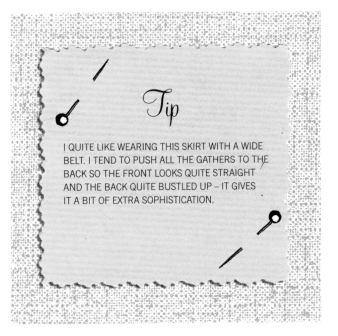

Tip

I QUITE LIKE WEARING THIS SKIRT WITH A WIDE BELT. I TEND TO PUSH ALL THE GATHERS TO THE BACK SO THE FRONT LOOKS QUITE STRAIGHT AND THE BACK QUITE BUSTLED UP – IT GIVES IT A BIT OF EXTRA SOPHISTICATION.

Machine-sew

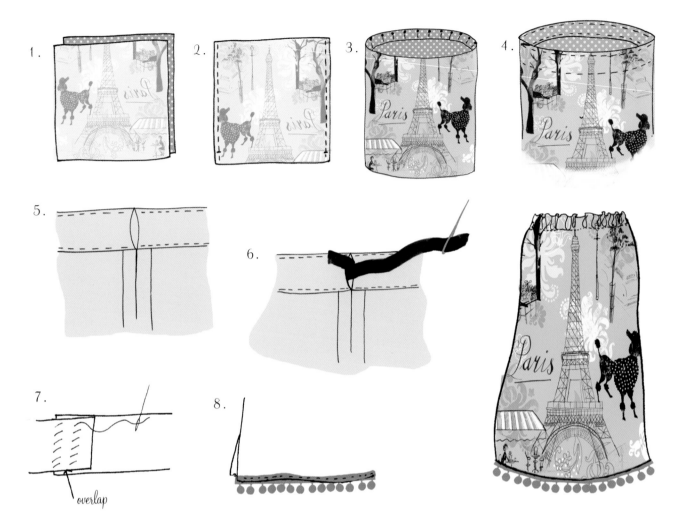

Pin the scarves together at the sides, with right sides of the scarves facing (1). Make sure you know which is the top and which is the bottom of the skirt. I find it helps to mark the top of the scarves by attaching a safety pin to them or marking with chalk.

Sew the sides together with a minimal seam allowance of around 5mm (2). Either sew up the sides completely, or leave the last 5cm or so on each side unsewn at the bottom for a slightly breezier feel. Using an iron, press the seams open and turn the skirt the right way out.

Fold over the top edge of the skirt to the inside by as much as you want and pin in place (3). I folded mine over by 6cm, but I could have folded over more to make the skirt shorter. Press this fold into the skirt and tack if you wish – the fabric can be slippery.

Stitch a line all round the skirt just below the folded top edge – this just gives a neat finish. Now sew a parallel line a few centimetres below it all the way round. You're making a channel wide enough for the elastic to slip through, so measure precisely (4).

Carefully open up the stitches on one of the inner side seams of the channel (5) and thread the elastic through the gap using a safety pin or bodkin (6). Once threaded, use a safety pin to pin the elastic together temporarily so you can try on your skirt to check the fit. Once happy, overlap the elastic and stitch together firmly (7).

Sew up the gap on the inner side seam by hand and strengthen the stitching where you opened up the seam by sewing a few simple stitches one on top of the other.

Stitch on any trims to the bottom of the skirt (8).

Bathtowel cover-up

Looking elegant on the beach may not be a problem for some, but for others (including me) it can be a bit of a challenge. Fortunately, I've been saved by this low-sew beauty. It's not only pretty, it's practical too, as the top doubles up as your beach towel.

To make this you'll need an average-sized bath towel – most are around 70cm wide and anything between 120cm and 140cm long, so the precise look of your top will depend on the dimensions. I've added a cosy contrasting kangaroo-style pocket for your hands that you can leave out if you wish. Personally though, especially on British beaches, I'm always glad of the additional warmth and I think it adds a little extra style. The top is trimmed with large buttons, the type you can cover in fabric. I've used towelling, but you can cover them in anything you wish.

This top is loose and generous, and should fit a UK size 10–16. Obviously it will be more roomy on the smaller figure. If you want a more fitted look, or are making a top for a child, then cut a few centimetres off either side of the towel to make it slightly narrower. A child will also need the neckline and armholes shortened a little.

I use a combination of hand and machine stitching, as the towelling can be easier at times to sew by hand. If you do likewise, a basic top will take you around an hour and a half to make. Adding the pocket and buttons will take an additional hour, but it's well worth it, I promise.

You'll need:

- ☐ Average-sized bath towel (see above)
- ☐ Measuring tape
- ☐ Pins
- ☐ Needle and thread
- ☐ Scissors
- ☐ Sewing machine
- ☐ Four cover buttons: I used two 3cm diameter and two 4cm diameter ones
- ☐ Scraps of fabric or towelling to cover buttons
- ☐ Another towel or piece of towelling fabric for contrasting pocket 28 x 42cm

1.

2.

3.

4.

5.

6.

7.

8.

9.

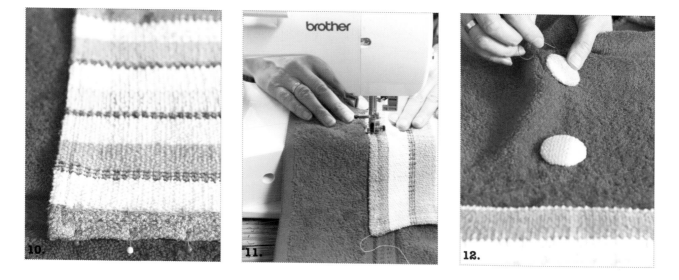

To make the hole for your head, fold the towel in half along its width. Measure along the folded edge to find the middle point. Mark with a pin. Measure 16cm either side of this point and cut straight along the fold. You should have a cut of 32cm in total (1).

To hem the neckline, start in the middle of the neckline and fold the edge back on to the wrong side by 1cm and then over again by 1cm, so the frayed edge is neatly tucked away – it will sort of roll into position (2). As you get towards the corners, the hem will naturally narrow. Pin in place and stitch down all the way around the neckline (3). Do this by hand as it is tricky with the sewing machine. Strengthen the corners with a few extra stitches too.

To make the armholes, fold the towel right sides together, with the neckline at the top. Place on a flat surface. Measure 30cm down from the top right-hand corner and put a pin in here as a marker (4). Stitch the towel together from this point down to the bottom edge with a 1cm hem allowance (5). Repeat for the left-hand side too. Turn the top the right way out. Fold the armhole edges under on to the wrong side by 1cm so they are even with the sides, pin and machine- or hand-stitch in place (6).

With the right sides of the top facing out, make a little 2cm tuck on either side of the middle point of the shoulder, right at the armhole edge (7). This will give the shoulders more shape. Pin in place and hold the tuck securely with a few hand stitches on either side and over the middle (8). Sew a 3cm covered button on top (9). Repeat for the other armhole.

For the pocket, first neaten all the pocket edges. Turn under by 2cm all the way round and machine-stitch along all four sides. Measuring carefully, position the pocket on the centre front of the top where it feels comfortable for your hands and pin in place (10). Stitch along the top and bottom edges of the pocket to attach it to the garment (11). Watch those pins if you're machine stitching. Finish off the front of the top by sewing on the two larger covered buttons (12).

Tips

IF YOU'RE USING NEW TOWELS, WASH THEM FIRST TO ALLOW FOR SHRINKAGE. ALSO IT'S BEST TO USE A TOWEL THAT ISN'T TOO FLUFFY AS THERE WILL BE TOO MUCH BULK. TOWELLING IS A BIT PRONE TO FRAYING, BUT ONCE YOU WASH IT A COUPLE OF TIMES YOUR TOP SHOULD BE FINE. ON THE PLUS SIDE, TOWELLING IS VERY FORGIVING OF LESS THAN PERFECT SEWING – IT ALL GETS HIDDEN IN THE FLUFFINESS!

Vintage collar and cuffs set

I love the idea of giving timeless, elegant clothes a magical temporary makeover for an evening. It's a mode of dressing that was very popular during the 'make-do and mend' years, when fashionable women had to be imaginative about how they made their slender wardrobes work overtime. I want to show you how to create this beautiful vintage-style lace collar and cuffs set. Stow it secretly in your overnight bag, and you'll be able to convert your classic black jumper, cardigan or dress into something a little more decadent when the occasion demands – as hopefully it will from time to time. The cuffs make cute bracelets in their own right, too.

To make this set you'll need the type of lace that comes already gathered. It's not expensive – I got it for under £1 per metre in my local haberdashery. I think it's normally used to trim nightdresses so it's usually made of a nylon mix.

I've used three different widths of lace to make the collar so that they layer up one on top of the other. Depending on the fullness of the gathers you may need to snip into the lace a little so that it lies flat on your neckline, an effect I rather like as it allows the other layers to peep through. I used just two layers of lace for the elasticated cuffs, to minimise bulk.

The collar is very simple so you'll complete it easily inside an hour using the sewing machine. You're just sewing lengths of lace on to the middle of a long ribbon, which you then tie around your neck in a bow.

The cuffs are a little trickier, and I use both hand sewing and the machine. Devote another hour and a half to making them. It will be time well spent. I've also included a very simple pair of glittering cuffs in the Tip. They're a speedy ten-minute alternative for girls on the go.

You'll need:

For both projects:

- ☐ Measuring tape
- ☐ Scissors
- ☐ Pins
- ☐ Needle and thread
- ☐ Sewing machine

For the collar:

- ☐ Three lengths of gathered lace of about 50–60cm, each a different width
- ☐ 1.5m ribbon or tape about 2.5cm wide (nothing too slippery, as it's harder to sew)
- ☐ Extra sequins or beads to trim

For the cuffs:

- ☐ Approx. 1m elastic slightly narrower than the ribbon
- ☐ 2m of ribbon or tape about 2.5cm wide (again nothing too slippery)
- ☐ Two lengths of gathered lace of about 1m, each a different width
- ☐ Iron
- ☐ Cloth, for pressing
- ☐ Bodkin or safety pin

Hand-sew   Machine-sew

For the collar:

Finally, pin the narrowest piece of lace right along the top edge of the ribbon. Make sure you don't see the edge of the ribbon peeking out beneath the lace as it will look a little messy. Tack if you wish and stitch down (4). Make sure you use a matching thread on this layer of lace, as any stitches will show. Remove all tacking stitches.

As you stitch, the lace may stretch a bit – don't worry about that too much. Just trim the lace as you work to make sure each piece is the same finished length (5).

Now try the collar on for size and tie with a bow. You can wear it with the bow to the back or the front. Trim the ribbon ends if needed and finish by cutting them on the diagonal. Snip into the lace if you find it's buckling (6) – it will ease it out a little.

Hand-sew sequins or beads to the collar for extra embellishment if you wish.

Collar

Measure around your neck (not too tight) and add on 6cm for ease. Cut the three lengths of lace to this measurement (1), and use a pin to mark the middle point along each of them.

Fold the ribbon in half to find its middle point too and mark with a little stitch in a contrasting colour. Put it flat on the table right side up. Take the widest piece of lace first and, matching the middle points, pin it right side up along the bottom of the ribbon as shown (2). Tack in place if you wish, or sew it directly to the ribbon with the machine, using whichever stitch you prefer (3). Watch those pins if you're sewing with the sewing machine. Remove them as you're sewing, if necessary.

Now take the next widest piece of lace and pin it on to the ribbon just above the first layer of lace in the same way as before. Tack, then stitch down.

Cuffs

Put on the outfit that the cuffs will go with and see where the sleeves finish. That's where your cuffs will go. Take the elastic and stretch it around your arm at this point to see how much you need. You want it to be taut enough to keep the cuff comfortably in place, but not so tight that it will stop your circulation. Add another 4cm to allow for overlap and adjustments. Get a friend to help with the measurement if needed. You can always cut the elastic down later when you do your final fitting, but you can't make it longer. Cut two pieces of elastic the same size, one for each cuff.

Use your original measurement for your arm (at the point where

the cuffs will be worn) and add another 12cm to the measurement. Cut four identical lengths of ribbon. You'll use two for each cuff.

Cut the lace to the same length as the ribbon – two pieces for each cuff in your two chosen widths.

To make up each cuff

Using the sewing machine, place two pieces of ribbon with right sides facing and stitch along one of the long sides leaving a 5mm seam allowance (1). Press the seam open (2).

Now take the wider piece of lace and machine-stitch it in place about half-way up the first section of ribbon (3). Of course, pin and tack in place beforehand if you feel happier doing that first. Take care not to let the foot get caught in the lace. Do the same with the narrower piece of lace, this time making sure the edge is right on the seam line (4). Use a matching thread here as the stitching will show.

For the cuffs:

Now fold the cuff in half with right sides together and sew the side seam up using a 1cm seam allowance (5). Press open, trim and fold over the ribbon. Press again using a damp cloth, if necessary, to make it as neat as possible (6).

Fold the lace out of the way and oversew the remaining open ribbon edge by hand (7), leaving a 2cm gap on either side of the seam.

Thread the elastic on to a bodkin or safety pin and pull through this gap, pinning to the edge of the cuff temporarily, if necessary, to stop it pinging out (8). Now overlap the ends of the elastic and pin them flat against each other. Make sure the elastic hasn't twisted inside. Try for size, adjust and, when you're happy with the fit, oversew the elastic by hand along the overlapping edges (9). Finally, oversew the remaining gap on the cuff, taking care not to catch the elastic as you work (10). Embellish if you wish. Wear with the seam on the inside of your arm. Repeat for the second cuff.

Tip

FOR A 10-MINUTE ALTERNATIVE, BUY A LENGTH OF WIDE, SEQUINNED ELASTIC AND SIMPLY WRAP AROUND YOUR ARM TO MEASURE THE AMOUNT FOR EACH CUFF. CUT, AND DAB A LITTLE CLEAR GLUE ON THE EDGES TO PREVENT FRAYING. SIMPLY TURN OVER ONE EDGE AND SEW IT FLAT ON TO THE OTHER EDGE. SLIP ON YOUR CUFFS. CHIC IN A FLASH!

Romantic lace scarf

This is a rather fabulous addition to any ladylike wardrobe. It's slightly flamboyant but very feminine at the same time, and wouldn't look out of place in a costume drama (with you or me playing opposite Mr Darcy of course!). It's a superb way of using up scraps of lace trim, and is really very simple to sew. It's actually quite warm on account of the foundation fabric (an old T-shirt) so it's a scarf that doesn't compromise on comfort either. Remember that the colour of the T-shirt will show through the lace, so choose something you like. If I were you, I wouldn't waste time pinning things in place in this project – it's not meant to be neat and tidy. You can patch up any mistakes with another bit of lace as you go. The one thing you need to watch though is that you don't pull the T-shirt as you sew. It will get out of shape because of the stretch in the fabric. Using a zigzag machine stitch for sewing on the lace will help. This scarf shouldn't take you more than a couple of hours at most.

You'll need:

- An old T-shirt (the larger the T-shirt, the longer and wider you can make your scarf)

- Scissors

- Sewing machine and thread

- Lots of lace scraps. You'll definitely need some longer lengths of lace trim, but you can also add in lace doilies or other lacy bits and bobs

Lay your T-shirt out flat. Cut right across the body just beneath the sleeves, then cut along one of the side seams. Cut off any labels and trim off any bulky bits. Open it out so it's one long strip (1).

Fold the strip in half along the length with wrong sides together. Now machine-stitch along the folded edge, about 1cm from the top, using a straight stitch (2). This folded edge will be the top edge of your scarf.

Open out the scarf again so the right sides are uppermost and keep them like this as you sew. You'll notice one half of the scarf has a finished edge (this was previously the bottom of the T-shirt) and one has a raw edge. You're going to sew all your lace scraps onto the half with the raw edge. The other half will act as a ready-made lining when it's folded back into place at the end. Remember to make sure your scarf is opened out at all times as you sew though – you don't want to stitch the two halves together by mistake.

Now take your first length or lengths of lace trim (they can be as long as you like) and machine-stitch onto the T-shirt so that they cover the raw bottom edge (3). Then simply sew successive overlapping lengths of lace onto the T-shirt (4). You can do this fairly randomly – but just remember that any unstitched edges of lace must all hang the same way – towards the raw bottom edge; otherwise when you put the scarf on, they'll fall the wrong way and expose the T-shirt.

Once you get to the folded top edge, make sure the final length of lace covers it nicely so that no-one will guess there's an old T-shirt acting as your foundation!

Stitch any doilies or other decoration to the scarf at the end – and you're done. Watch out Mr Darcy!

Everlasting thank-you flowers

I can't claim to have dreamt these up. I once saw them decorating the front window of Anthropologie in New York, and worked out how to make my own. My guess is that they originate in the shanty towns where people defy their dismal surroundings to create beautiful objects from scrap to earn a bit of money. These flowers make a wonderful present for a kind host or hostess, and what's even better is that they last forever and look great in the garden. If you're feeling generous, give the money you will save from buying real flowers to a charity of your choice – and pass the good will on.

You can rustle up a bunch of these flowers within an hour. There are two types of flower here – of course you can make up more of your own!

Nothing beats a big bunch of beautiful blooms when it comes to expressing gratitude. So although these flowers aren't fashion accessories I'm sneaking them in as a way of saying a big THANK YOU to everyone who helped make this book happen. Enjoy and pass on!

You'll need:

- ☐ Plastic drinks bottles cleaned with the caps and labels removed
- ☐ Scissors
- ☐ Spray paint for plastic
- ☐ Glitter (optional)
- ☐ Some old newspaper
- ☐ Garden wire and wire cutters

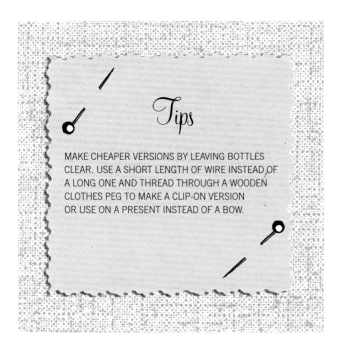

Tips

MAKE CHEAPER VERSIONS BY LEAVING BOTTLES CLEAR. USE A SHORT LENGTH OF WIRE INSTEAD OF A LONG ONE AND THREAD THROUGH A WOODEN CLOTHES PEG TO MAKE A CLIP-ON VERSION OR USE ON A PRESENT INSTEAD OF A BOW.

Cut off the top third of the bottles and recycle the rest.

Flower one is simple to create as you're making straight petals. Just cut parallel lines about 1cm apart into the plastic towards the neck of the bottle (nozzle). Bend all the 'petals' outwards to create your flower. You can see from the picture that I've varied this a bit by cutting some of the 'petals' shorter than the others.

Flower two is a little bit more tricky as you're making stamens and petals. Again working towards the neck of the bottle, cut a pointed petal shape into the plastic. Then move round the bottle and cut another petal shape, but importantly, make sure the petals don't touch each other. You want about a 1cm gap between them at their widest point. Work your way around the bottle, using your judgement to get the petals fairly evenly spaced. Now bend the pointed petals outwards. You'll be left with stamens in the middle, which you can trim back to whatever size you prefer.

Now for glamming the flowers up! Put them on to some newspaper and spray following the instructions on the can – you should do this outside. Mix colours for unique effects. Sprinkle glitter on to the paint whilst still tacky. Leave to dry.

To make the stems, cut a length of garden wire about 35cm long and wrap the end of it around the bottle neck. Turn up the sharp point of the wire for safety.

No-sew

templates

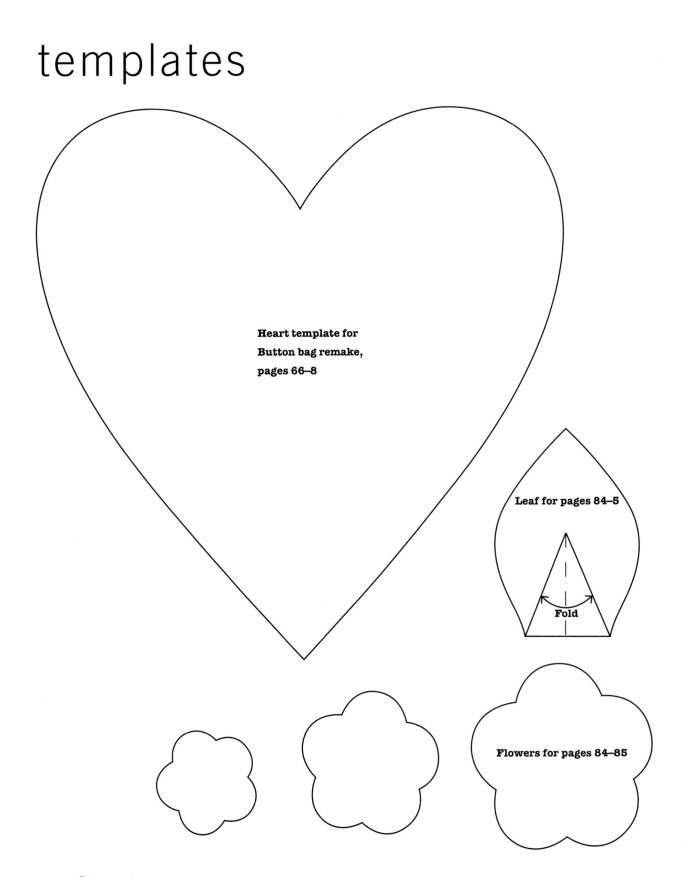

Heart template for
Button bag remake,
pages 66–8

Leaf for pages 84–5

Fold

Flowers for pages 84–85

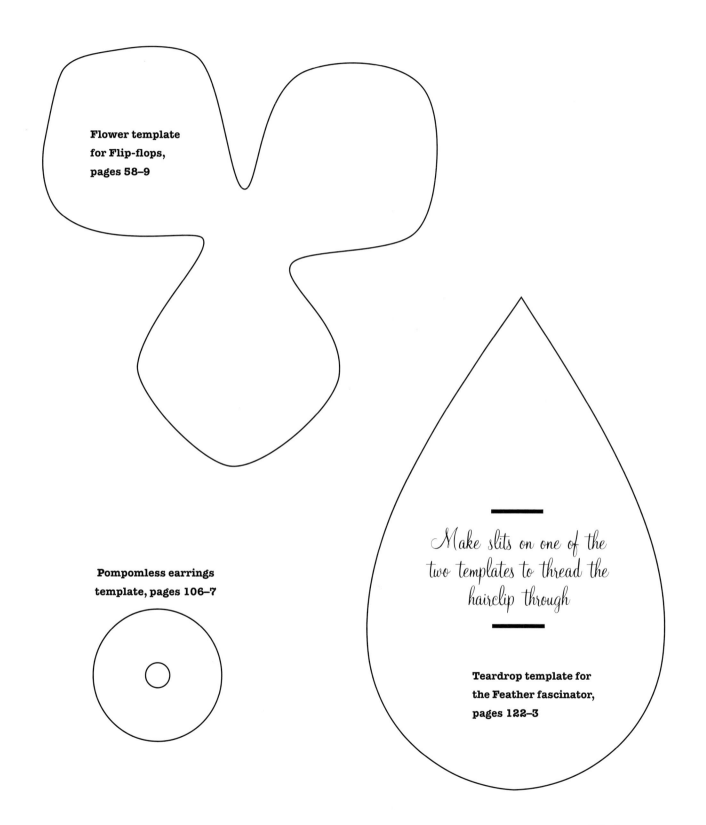

Flower template
for Flip-flops,
pages 58–9

Pompomless earrings
template, pages 106–7

Make slits on one of the
two templates to thread the
hairclip through

Teardrop template for
the Feather fascinator,
pages 122–3

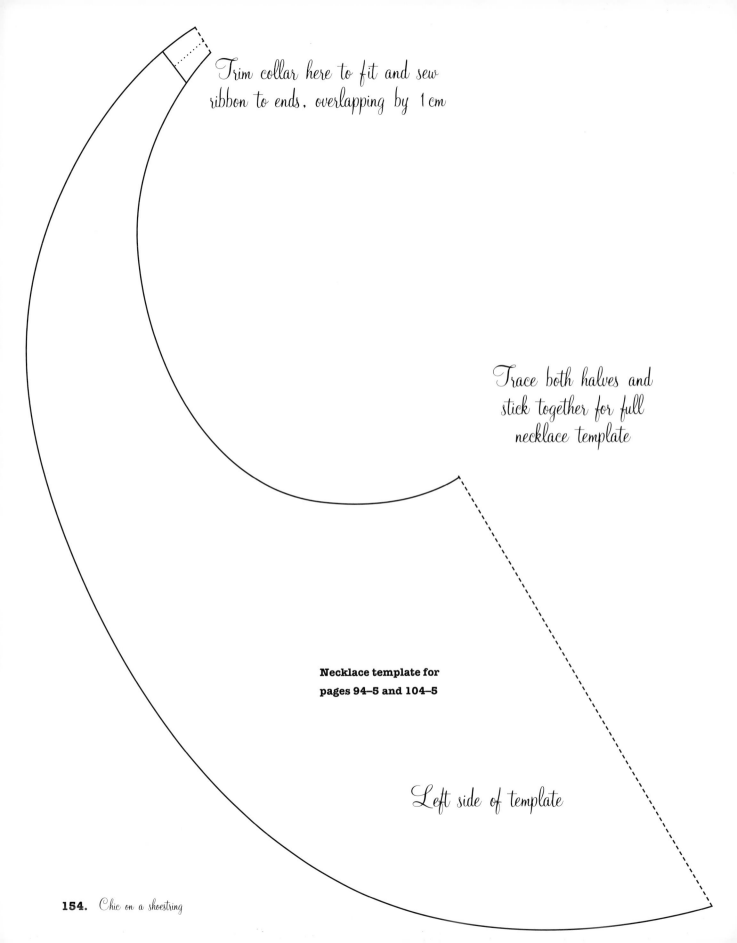

Trim collar here to fit and sew
ribbon to ends, overlapping by 1 cm

Trace both halves and
stick together for full
necklace template

**Necklace template for
pages 94–5 and 104–5**

Left side of template

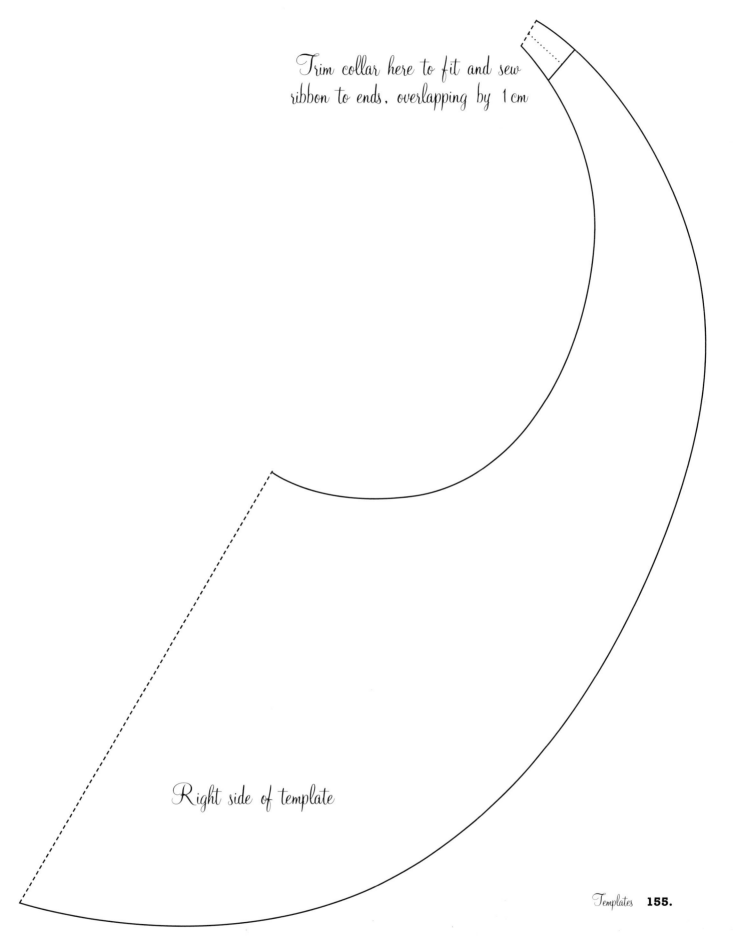

Trim collar here to fit and sew
ribbon to ends, overlapping by 1 cm

Right side of template

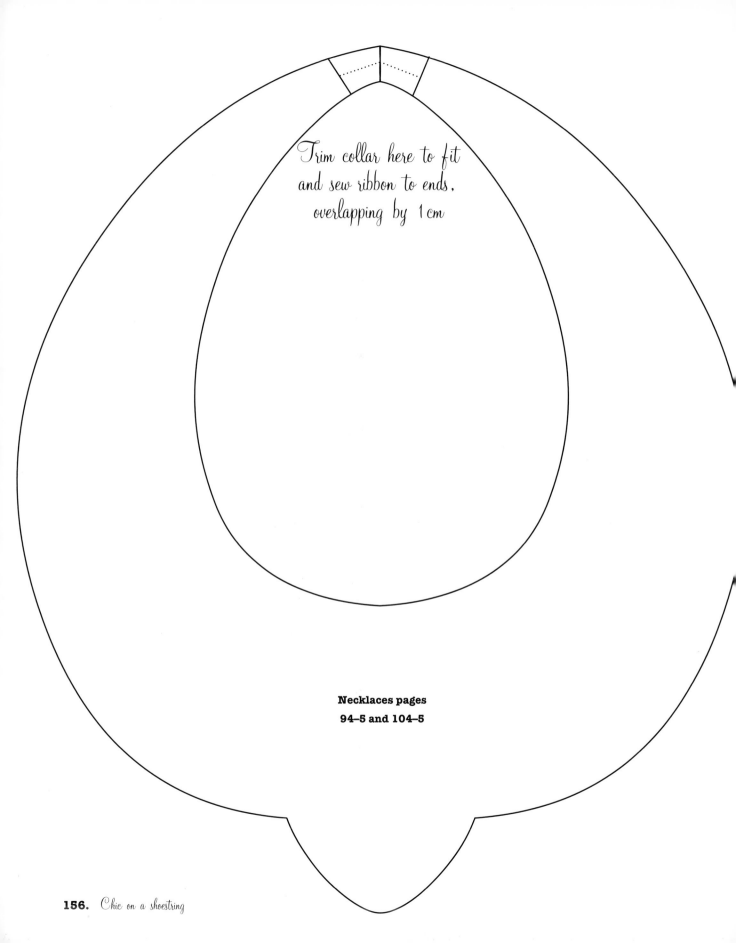

Trim collar here to fit
and sew ribbon to ends,
overlapping by 1 cm

Necklaces pages
94–5 and 104–5

suppliers

Some suppliers of beautiful things:

Andrew Hirst
Wayward Vintage Fabric & Trims
58 Norman Road
St Leonards on Sea
TN38 0EJ
and also
Stand 159, Portobello Road, London
www.waywardvintagefabric.com

Artnuptia
32 Rue N D des Victoires, 75002 Paris, France
+33 1 42 36 06 75
www.artnuptia.free.fr
Lovely flowers and hat-making supplies. Some vintage.

Barnett Lawson Trimmings Ltd
www.bltrimmings.com
London – treasure trove of haberdashery supplies at trade prices

Berger Beads Specialty Company
www.bergerbeads.net
Great for vintage sequins, beads, findings – based in the US

Daniel et Lili
Marche Dauphine – stand 128
140, rue des Rosiers, 93400 St Ouen, France
www.daniel-et-lili.net
Fabulous place in the St Ouen flea market in Paris,
full of vintage finds

Duttons for Buttons
www.duttonsforbuttons.co.uk
Buttons of all sorts and haberdashery in Yorkshire, UK

Liberty
www.liberty.co.uk
Great haberdashery department, and chic shopping!

Many Horses Jewellery Supply
www.manyhorses.com
Great for extra long hatpins

Milliner Warehouse
www.millinerwarehouse.co.uk
Millinery suppliers in London

Sequin appliqués
www.sequinappliques.com/store
As it says on the tin!

Temptation Alley
www.temptationalley.com
London – trimmings at wholesale prices

Top Trimmings Ltd
www.toptrimming.com
All sorts of wonderful large sew-on sparkles, and other fabulous
finds in New York.

Supplier of metal studs
http://stores.ebay.com/DENK-Studs-Beads-and-Crafts

Also look out for your local haberdasher –
mine is Peter and Joan,
119 Deptford High Street
London
SE8 4NS

index

acknowledgments

It's always so difficult to know who to make special reference to when you recall just how many people have helped you write a book. So in the words of one of my heroines, Maria from The Sound of Music, 'I'll start at the very beginning,' as it's always a very good place to start.

Making Christmas cards at the dining room table with my Mum and brothers is one of my happiest early memories. Glitter and cotton wool must have been everywhere! My parents believed in encouraging their children to be creative and imaginative. They both died some time ago. I still miss them very much, and have dedicated this book to them.

My brothers Anthony and Christopher are two of my best friends, and have always been behind me 100% through life's many ups and downs. I'm hugely grateful to them for their sustained and loving support.

Many thanks to the team at Kyle Cathie, especially to Kyle herself for seeing something different and backing it, and to Sophie Allen, my editor, whose patience, enthusiasm and commitment has been incredible.

I owe huge thanks to Louise Leffler, who's designed a book that has more than a touch of magic about it, seamlessly marrying together the beautiful work of photographer Claire Richardson and illustrator Sam Wilson. Collaborating with all these talented women has been a complete joy. Amy Barton and Carol Morley also deserve special thanks for their creative input, as do my fabulous models Francesca Forman and Charlotte Leffler. I'm grateful to Ali Allen who made us welcome in her lovely home in spite of a new baby to tend to. Her paintings feature extensively throughout the book providing a stylish backdrop to many of the photographs.

I'd also like to thank my literary agent Clare Hulton who spotted the potential of Chic on a Shoestring, and thank you too to Miranda Holt, who introduced me to Clare right at the start.

There are so many people who've helped and supported me over the years. In particular, Sandra Westbrooke, a former BBC colleague and dear friend, has been there both emotionally and practically throughout the writing of Chic on a Shoestring. She stitched and listened as the book took shape, and her involvement has been invaluable. She even passed on to me a stash of beautiful embellishments left to her by her friend Beryl Whiteley. I'm so happy to have been able to put them to good use. Sandra's husband John has been a real treasure too, offering his editor's eye for free. Debbi Kinrade deserves a special mention for galvanising me into action. Her wise counsel has been invaluable during many highs and lows. Rene Wyndham too has always been a real cheerleader for my work.

Julia Davies, Helen Tate, Katharina Hock, Iris Debremaeker, Catarina Walsh, Fiona Maida, Robert Maida, Melanie Abbott, Oana Lungescu, Kate Poyser, Kelvin Brown, Natasha Gruneberg, Luisa Baldini, Martha Dixon, Judy Fladmark, Georgina Worthington, Geoff Goff, Yolanda Vega, Joanna Kelly, Emilie Fjola, Kamilla Weinhart, Kirsten Scott, Gina Foster, Alba Castillo, Veronique Tissieres, Paula Rice, Louise Presley, Elspeth Reid, Jennifer Mair, Josephine Steed, Pippa Sandison, Robert Wignall, Paula Williams, Giles Laverack, Fiona Guest, Sarah Roberts, Ailsa McCarthy, Manon Davies, Sofia Connolly, Helen Shields, John McManus, Betty Redondo, Yo Haniewicz, Amanda Kirton, Mandy Stokes, Sarah Whitehead, Mark Perrow, Simon Enright, Robin Punt, Jonathan Paterson, Malcolm Downing, Peter Bestwick, Peter Owen, Iain Croft, Marcia Mascoll, Krassi Hendry, Joanne Cayford, Jane Warr, Elaine Hooley, Bridget Sojourner, Nicola Jackson, Robin Ross and Mike Duran. All these people have played very special roles in encouraging me to carry on when things got tough. I'd also like to include here my lovely friend Merryn Butler who died suddenly and unexpectedly before this book was published. She would smile to see it.

To all these people and many other friends and BBC colleagues – I am extremely grateful. Without your help and support I couldn't have done it.

THANK YOU. Mary Jane Baxter. London, December 2010.